$ \# $ + $ - $ \% $ ¾ $ \sim \$^2

Money Math
Lessons for Life

written by
Mary C. Suiter
Sarapage McCorkle
Center for Entrepreneurship & Economic Education
University of Missouri-St. Louis

mathematics consultant
Helene J. Sherman
University of Missouri-St. Louis

cover design by
Sandy Morris

sponsored by

AFSA Education Foundation
Coinstar Inc.
Department of the Treasury
The Fannie Mae Foundation
Eastman Kodak Company
Merrill Lynch & Co.
The Mohegan Tribe
The Nasdaq Stock Market, Inc.
University of Missouri-St. Louis

American Payroll Association
Consumer Credit Counseling Service-St. Louis
Deutsche Bank Americas Foundation
Jump$tart Coalition for Personal Financial Literacy
Lockheed Martin Corporation
Metropolitan Life Foundation
Museum of American Financial History
National Association of Securities Dealers, Inc.
Verizon Foundation

$\$^3 = $ ¢ $ ½ $ + $ \infty $ \ni $

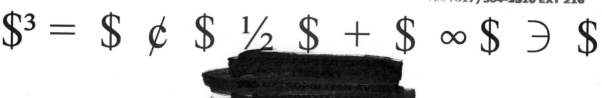

The authors thank the following sponsors for supporting this important project.

AFSA Education Foundation
Coinstar Inc.
Department of the Treasury
The Fannie Mae Foundation
Eastman Kodak Company
Merrill Lynch & Co.
The Mohegan Tribe
The Nasdaq Stock Market, Inc.
University of Missouri-St. Louis

American Payroll Association
Consumer Credit Counseling Service-St. Louis
Deutsche Bank Americas Foundation
Jump$tart Coalition for Personal Financial Literacy
Lockheed Martin Corporation
Metropolitan Life Foundation
Museum of American Financial History
National Association of Securities Dealers, Inc.
Verizon Foundation

The authors are grateful to the following pilot teachers and reviewers for their feedback.

Tom Brann
North County Middle School
North St. Francois County R-1

Gayla Brinkley
West County R-IV Middle School
West County R-IV District

Pamela Cornwell
Holman Middle School
Pattonville School District

Helen Fields
Holman Middle School
Pattonville School District

Freda I. Hill
Compton-Drew ILC Middle
St. Louis Public Schools

Ken Hunott
Berkeley Middle School
Ferguson-Florissant School District

Sharon McNeil
Berkeley Middle School
Ferguson-Florissant School District

Dean Penberthy
Compton-Drew ILC Middle
St. Louis Public Schools

Susan Reid
Compton-Drew ILC Middle
St. Louis Public Schools

Jay Walsh
Barbara McNair Elementary School
University City School District

John Clow, Director
Leatherstocking Center for Economic Education
College at Oneonta Department of Economics & Business
State University of New York

Barbara Flowers, Assistant Director
Center for Entrepreneurship & Economic Education
University of Missouri-St. Louis

Foreword . . . . **vii**

Introduction . . . . **ix**

Lesson 1   The Secret to Becoming a Millionaire **1**

Students learn how saving helps people become wealthy. They develop "rules to become a millionaire" as they work through a series of exercises, learning that it is important to: (1) save early and often, (2) save as much as possible, (3) earn compound interest, (4) try to earn a high interest rate, (5) leave deposits and interest earned in the account as long as possible, and (6) choose accounts for which interest is compounded often. This lesson assumes that students have worked with percents and decimal equivalents.

.Lesson 2   Wallpaper Woes **25**

Students hear a story about Tom, a middle-school student who wants to redecorate his bedroom. They measure the classroom wall dimensions, draw a scale model, and incorporate measurements for windows and doors to determine the area that could be covered by wallpaper. Students then hear more about Tom's redecorating adventure, learning about expenses, budget constraints, and trade-offs. For assessment, students measure their rooms at home. This lesson requires that students know how to measure, or a review may be necessary before teaching.

Lesson 3   Math and Taxes: A Pair to Count On **39**

Students examine careers and reflect on how workers use math in their occupations. They study selected occupations, learning about the work skills (human capital) that different workers possess and salaries that those workers earn. Next, students learn about how taxes are paid on income that people earn and how income tax is calculated. They learn how the progressive federal income tax is based on the ability-to-pay principle.

Lesson 4   Spreading the Budget **67**

Students develop a budget for a college student, using a spreadsheet. They examine the student's fixed, variable, and periodic expenses and revise to adjust for cash flow problems that appear on the first spreadsheet. This lesson is designed to increase student awareness and appreciation of the efficiency of using computer technology in math applications.

Learning how to manage money is part of becoming a responsible adult but a recent national study conducted by the ***Jump$tart Coalition for Personal Financial Literacy*** has shown that there is an appalling ignorance of monetary concepts among high school seniors. This test measured financial literacy and resulted in an average score of 51.9%, a failing grade on a typical scale. The study concluded that America's young adults are leaving high schools without the ability to make critical financial decisions affecting their lives. Many are unable to balance a checkbook and most simply have no insight into the basic survival principles involved with credit card usage, saving, and investing.

Even though personal finance is a life skill like reading and writing, it is often not considered as such in our nation's school curriculum. The Jump$tart study found that only 12% of the respondents said they learned about personal finance while in school. Since personal finance is primarily taught in classes that are electives like Business or Family and Consumer Science, the integration of personal finance concepts into other relevant classes such as mathematics and economics, which are more mainstream, is integral.

Without adequate personal finance education while in school, students are forced to either learn from their parents, who may not be providing the best example, or to learn by the costly alternative—the trial-and-error method. This second method is dangerous since personal finance has evolved into a complex life skill requiring more self-direction than ever before. For example, credit is now widely available to young adults. In fact, it is no longer necessary to have a job or any credit history to be issued credit. In addition, new entrants into the workforce are increasingly being asked retirement questions such as, "which funds they want to invest in and at what percentage." The urgency for personal finance instruction has never been greater.

Without proper education in personal finance, today's young students may become tomorrow's bankruptcy candidates. Too often, parents find their adult children back on their doorstep (because of financial problems) instead of leaving the nest for good. This scenario and other similarly distressing ones can be avoided if young adults have the skills necessary to make informed financial decisions. *Money Math: Lessons for Life* is a proven way to start our young adults off on the right path to financial literacy.

Dara Duguay
Executive Director
Jump$tart Coalition for Personal Financial Literacy

The lessons contained in this packet are the result of the joining together of resources from the U.S. government, corporations, a university and non-profit organizations to bring basic financial concepts into the classroom through mathematics. Beyond presenting key basic personal finance concepts through math, which is a core subject, the authors and partners wanted the lessons to target middle-school students, so that these students could start to learn these concepts earlier and build on them throughout their teen years. Three years ago these lessons were just a concept. Now, all U.S. teachers have the means to incorporate real-world financial scenarios in their classrooms, initiating this life-long process earlier.

The partnership that brought about the lessons fits the definition of a true partnership. Each participant was committed to the goal of offering resources to teachers who want to teach personal finance skills to their students. Furthermore, as the project progressed and took shape, the partnering organizations pitched in to provide whatever was needed to move forward. An excellent final product has resulted from the partnership that combined the wisdom and strengths of individuals and organizations – all contributing their time, resources and perspectives to this project. Thank you to all of the partners and individuals who invested in and were committed to *Money Math: Lessons for Life* throughout these past years.

Robin Francis
U.S. Department of the Treasury

Lesson Description	Students learn how saving helps people become wealthy. They develop "rules to become a millionaire" as they work through a series of exercises, learning that it is important to: (1) save early and often, (2) save as much as possible, (3) earn compound interest, (4) try to earn a high interest rate, (5) leave deposits and interest earned in the account as long as possible, and (6) choose accounts for which interest is compounded often. This lesson assumes that students have worked with percents and decimal equivalents.
Objectives	Students will be able to: 1. define saving, incentive, interest, and opportunity cost. 2. solve problems using interest rate, fractions, decimals, and percentages. 3. calculate compound interest. 4. explain the benefits of compound interest. 5. explain the opportunity cost of saving 6. describe a savings bond investment.
Mathematics Concepts	percent, decimal, data analysis, number sense, solving equations, problem solving
Personal Finance Concepts	interest, interest rate, compounding, wealth, saving, savings, inflation, purchasing power
Materials Required	• copies of Activities 1-1 through 1-5 for each student • transparencies of Visuals 1-1 through 1-7 • calculator for each student • computers
Time Required	4 - 6 days
Procedure	**Get Ready** 1. Ask the following. Do you want to be a millionaire? What is a millionaire? Explain that a **millionaire** is a person who has wealth totaling one or more million dollars, noting that **wealth** is the total value of what a person owns minus what he or she owes. How could you become a millionaire? (*win the lottery, win a sweepstakes, inherit a million dollars, earn a high income*) Read the following scenario to the class.

1

Last week, Mrs. Addle told her students that they could become millionaires if they followed the rules she provided them. As a matter of fact, she guaranteed that if they followed her rules exactly, they would be millionaires in 47 years! Misha and the rest of her classmates thought that Mrs. Addle was crazy. If she had rules that would guarantee that someone could be a millionaire, why was she teaching seventh-grade math? Why wasn't she rich and retired? Why didn't she follow her own rules? Mrs. Addle told the students to go home and talk to their families about what she had said.

Misha went home and told her family what Mrs. Addle had said. Misha's mother knew a lot about money and financial matters. She just smiled at Misha and said that Mrs. Addle was correct. When Misha returned to class the next day, Mrs. Addle asked what the students' families said. Of the 25 students in Mrs. Addle's class, 20 students said that their parents and other family members agreed with Mrs. Addle. The other five students forgot to ask.

2. Explain that to learn more about being a millionaire, the students first must review what a percent is. (Note: If needed, Visual 1-1 includes a review.)

3. Point out that in the story, there are 25 students in Misha's class, and 20 students discovered that their families agreed with Mrs. Addle. Ask the following questions. (Note: Step-by-step calculations are provided on Visual 1-2.)

    a. What percent of the students' families thought that Mrs. Addle was correct? (*80%*)
    b. What percent of the students failed to do their homework? (*20%*)

Get Going

1. Explain that you will share Mrs. Addle's secrets with them. When they become millionaires, they can donate money to the school's math department! Discuss the following.

a. How do you earn income? (*mow lawns, baby-sit, walk pets, rake leaves, do chores around the house*)

b. What do you do with your income? (*save it, spend it, save some and spend some*)

c. Why do you spend your income? (*to buy things that they want now, such as movies, food, and clothes*)

d. Why do you save your income? (*to buy things they want in the future*)

2. Explain that when people earn income, they can spend it or save it. When they are **spending**, they spend their money today for goods and services, but they give up the chance to have goods and services in the future. When **saving**, they give up goods and services now to have other goods and services in the future. When people make choices, the highest-valued alternative choice that is given up is their **opportunity cost**. Read the following scenario.

   Next year, you want to take a family and consumer science class, a woodworking class, and a photography class. However, you only have room in your schedule for one of these three. Which would you choose? What would be your second choice?

3. Have several students share their first and second choices. Explain that their second choice is their opportunity cost — it is the highest-valued alternative class. When people save, the goods and services that they would have purchased now — the highest-valued alternative — represent their opportunity cost. When they spend now, their opportunity cost is goods and services they could have in the future.

4. Assign Activity 1-1. When they are finished, have students share answers. (*1. $360, $720, $1080, $1440, $1800, $2160; 2. The items they would have purchased each day with $2. This is their opportunity cost. 3. A + (B x 180) where A = previous year balance and B = the amount deposited each day; 4. Save more each day.*) Point out that students have different opportunity costs because their tastes and priorities are different.

5. Display Visual 1-3. Have students deduce what has changed in each case. They should develop Rules 1 and 2 to become a millionaire. (*In the first case, the saver is saving for a longer period; therefore, Millionaire Rule 1 is to start saving early. In the second case, the saver is saving $4 per day instead of $2 per day; therefore, Millionaire Rule 2 is to save more or to save as much as possible.*) Write the two rules on the board.

6. Discuss the following.

   a. How many of you have savings accounts in banks? (*Answers will vary.*)
   b. What are the benefits of placing your savings in a bank? (*The money is safe in the bank, and the bank pays interest.*)
   c. What is interest? (*Students may or may not know the exact definition of interest.*)

7. For homework, students who have savings accounts may bring in a statement from their savings accounts. Have all students look for ads in local newspapers and listen to television and radio ads about banks. Tell them to write down any information about interest rates.

Keep It Going

1. Assign Activity 1-2. Allow students to share their answers. (*1. $396, $831.60, $1310.76, $1837.84, $2417.62, $3055.38; 2. (A+360) + [(A+360) x .10] where A is the previous year's ending balance, or, 1.10 (A+360); 3. These amounts are higher because they earn interest on the deposit and interest on the interest earned in previous years.*)

2. Point out that the 10% amount that Uncle Mort pays is an incentive. An **incentive** is a reward that encourages people to behave in a particular way. This incentive encourages people to save and keep their savings. How much of an incentive did Uncle Mort pay the first year? (*$360 x .10 = $36*)

3. Explain that banks provide an incentive for people to save. When people make deposits to savings accounts, banks are able to use the money to loan to others. In return, the banks pay

Teaching Tip:

Show students how just a little bit of money can add up to a lot of cash with careful saving and investing. Ask your students to save their pocket change for one month.

Assuming your students save $1 a day, they should have $30 after one month of saving. If your students invest $30 worth of change every month for 10 years, how much money will they have if they invest their money in the following ways:

▪ Savings account with a 2% annual rate of return

▪ Money market fund with a 5% annual rate of return

▪ Mutual fund with a 9% annual rate of return

What can your students buy with this money? Will it be enough to purchase a car when they turn 22?

interest to savers. **Interest** is a payment for the use of money. Bankers don't usually tell people that they will earn a specific sum of money. Savers are told the interest rate to be received. The **interest rate** is the annual interest payment on an amount expressed as a percentage. For example, a bank might pay a 4% interest rate on a savings account. Uncle Mort pays 10%.

4. Write the word "compounding" on the board. Ask students what they think this word means and how it applies to becoming a millionaire. Allow students to look the word up in the dictionary and in newspaper advertisements. Guide students to recognize that leaving interest earned on savings in the savings account so that the saver earns interest on the original deposit and interest on the interest is called earning **compound interest**. Have students develop Millionaire Rule 3 and write it on the board. (*Earn compound interest.*)

5. Explain that banks pay compound interest on savings, although it may not be as much as Uncle Mort pays. Discuss the following.

   a. Give examples of the interest rates local banks are paying from the statements, ads, and ad information brought from home. (*Answers will vary; however, the rates are likely to be much lower than the 10% that Uncle Mort pays.*)
   b. What would happen to the amount of accumulated savings if Uncle Mort paid only 5%? (*It would decrease.*)

6. Display Visual 1-4. Explain that this table illustrates what would happen if a bank paid 5% interest compounded annually. Point out that comparing the savings results at 5% with the savings results for 10% (*$2571.12 at 5% compared to $3055.78 at 10%*) gives us another rule for becoming a millionaire. Discuss the following.

   a. Based on the comparison between accumulated savings with 5% interest and with 10% interest, what is the fourth rule of becoming a millionaire? (*Try to earn a high interest rate.*) Add this rule to the list on the board.
   b. What would happen to accumulated savings if the deposits and interest were left in the account, earning 5% interest for another six years? (*It would increase.*)

c.   What is the fifth rule of becoming a millionaire? (*Leave deposits and interest in the account for as long as possible.*) Add this rule to the board.

7.   Have students consider how they used their calculators to solve these problems. Guide them to develop a recursive equation such as [ANS + 0.05(ANS)] = ending balance for each year or [ANS + 0.05(ANS)] + 360 = beginning balance for each successive year.

8.   Review the basic rules for becoming a millionaire. Write the following rules on the board.
   (1) Save early and often.
   (2) Save as much as possible.
   (3) Earn compound interest.
   (4) Try to earn a high interest rate.
   (5) Leave deposits and interest in the account as long as possible.

Graph It (Optional)

1.   Tell students they will create four line graphs on the same set of axes. These graphs should show the amount of savings earned over time: (a) when saving $360 per year for six years in a bank, (b) when saving $360 for 10 years in a bank, (c) when saving $720 per year for six years, and (3) when saving $360 per year for six years at a 5% interest rate per year. They determine the dependent and independent variables and label the axes appropriately. They should retain these graphs for later use. They may use a graphing calculator, a computer, or paper and pencil to create the graphs.

2.   Have students create a circle graph that shows the percent of total savings that resulted from deposits by the saver and the percent that resulted from compound interest when saving $360 per year for six years at a 5% interest rate. They may use a graphing calculator, a computer, or paper, pencil, and a protractor.

Check It — Assessment

Display Visual 1-4, and assign Activity 1-3 to each student. When students are finished, display Visual 1-5 so they can check their answers.

Keep Going

1. Have students refer to the savings account and advertisement information they brought from home. Discuss the following.

    a. Do the ads or account statements tell consumers that the interest rate is compounded annually? Semi-annually? Quarterly? (*Answers will vary.*)
    b. What do you think these terms mean? (*annually - once per year; semi-annually - twice per year; quarterly - four times per year*)
    c. How do you think semi-annual or quarterly compounding might affect accumulated savings? (*Answers may vary.*)
    d. How do you think quarterly interest payments would be calculated? (*Answers may vary.*)

2. Assign Activity 1-4 to groups of 4 or 5 students. Tell the groups to work together to complete the activity. Display Visual 1-6 to check and correct their answers.

3. Display Visual 1-4 again. Ask students to compare this table with the quarterly compound table they completed. Discuss the following.

    a. What was the total amount deposited by the saver in each case? (*$2160*)
    b. How much interest was earned with interest compounded annually? (*$411.12*)
    c. How much interest was earned with interest compounded quarterly? (*$419.54*)
    d. How much additional interest was earned through quarterly compounding? (*$8.42*)
    e. What do you think would happen if interest were compounded daily? (*more accumulated savings at the end of the year*)

Teaching Tip:

Be sure to tell your students that people put their savings in many places. Many people choose to invest their savings in stocks. Buying stocks means buying some ownership (equity) in a company. On average, over time, stocks have earned higher returns than savings accounts. Stockholders receive returns from dividends (a portion of business profit paid to stockholders) and capital gains (the amount of the sale of stock that exceeds the original price paid by the stockholder).

Tell students to look at the stock tables in the financial pages of a newspaper. Point out that the yield (Yld) is the return from dividends stated as a percentage. Have students compare the dividend yield to interest rates on savings accounts. Then, point out that most stock investors are interested in capital gains; that is, the increased value of the stock from the time it was purchased. Have students research how much stocks, on average, have increased over time. Information on the growth of the S&P 500 can be found at the following web site.

http://www.nasdaq.com/ services/pf_university.stm

Click on "Investing 101," then click on "The Odds Are In Your Favor" under "Why It Works.

f. What is the sixth and final rule for becoming a millionaire? (*Deposit money in accounts for which interest is compounded most often.*) Add the rule to the list on the board.

4. Review all rules to becoming a millionaire.

    (1) Save early and often.
    (2) Save as much as possible.
    (3) Earn compound interest.
    (4) Leave deposits and interest in the account for as long as possible.
    (5) Try to earn high interest rates.
    (6) Choose accounts for which interest is compounded often.

Compute It

1. Divide students into pairs. Explain that their task is to discover combinations of interest rate, deposit, and years of savings will lead to the goal of becoming millionaires. They may use a financial calculator, spreadsheet financial functions on the computer, or visit www.financenter.com and use the financial calculator.

2. Once they have decided what program to use, they should enter various combinations of deposit amounts, interest rates, years of saving, and how often interest is compounded and note the impact on accumulated savings.

3. Have student pairs share the combinations with which they would be happiest. Discuss whether these combinations are realistic with questions such as "Is it reasonable to expect an interest rate of 20%?" or "What amount of monthly income do you think a person must earn in order to save $3000 per month?"

Wrap It Up

Discuss the following to highlight important information.

1. What does a percentage represent? (*some part of a hundred*)

2. How can 55% be expressed as a decimal? *(.55)* a fraction? *(55/100)*
3. What is interest? *(payment for the use of money)*
4. What is an interest rate? *(the annual interest payment on an account expressed as a percentage)*
5. What is compounding? *(paying interest on previous interest)*
6. What is saving? *(income not spent today to be able to buy goods and services in the future)*
7. What is opportunity cost? *(the highest-valued alternative that is given up)*
8. What is the opportunity cost of saving? *(goods and services given up today)*
9. What are some rules about saving that can help you become a millionaire? *(Start saving early and save regularly. Save as much as you can. Leave the deposit and interest earned in the account as long as possible. Try to earn a high interest rate. Seek savings options that compound interest often.)*

Check It/Write It — Assessment

Explain that students' work with the computer or calculator helped them see the impact of the various rules on the quest to become a millionaire. Divide the students into small groups and tell them to answer the following questions in writing, as a group.

1. What happens to accumulated savings if the deposit amount increases? *(Savings would increase. Saving larger amounts generates greater savings in the future.)*
2. What happens to accumulated savings if the interest rate increases? *(It would increase.)*
3. What happens to accumulated savings if the number of compounding periods per year increases? Why? *(It would increase because every time compounding occurs, the saver is earning interest on interest earned.)*
4. What happens to accumulated savings if the number of years increases? *(It would increase.)*
5. What is the key to becoming a millionaire? *(Save as much as possible for as long as possible earning a high interest rate that is compounded frequently.)*

Going Beyond — A Challenge Activity

1. Remind students that one of the important rules about saving is to try to earn a high interest rate. To do that, savers must investigate various savings options available. If people save in a piggy bank, they don't earn any interest on their savings, and it isn't particularly safe. If people place their savings in a savings account at the bank, they earn interest and it is usually safe because of deposit insurance. However, the interest rate is usually lower on these accounts than some other savings options.

2. Explain that people can put their money in a certificate of deposit or CD. A certificate of deposit is a savings account that pays higher interest than a regular bank savings account. However, when people put their money in a CD, they promise to leave the savings in the account for a certain amount of time, such as six months, a year, or five years.

3. Explain that many people save by buying savings bonds issued by the United States government. When people buy a savings bond, they are lending money to the government to help finance programs or projects. Savings bonds come in different denominations, such as $50, $100, or $500. They are considered to be a very safe way to save money; that is, they are virtually risk-free.

4. Point out that the newest type of U.S. savings bond is the I Bond. I Bonds are inflation-indexed and designed for savers who want to protect themselves from inflation. Define **inflation** as an increase in the average level of prices in the economy. (A simpler definition is an increase in most prices.)

5. Explain that inflation reduces the purchasing power of savings. **Purchasing power** is the ability to buy things with an amount of money. People save because they want to buy things in the future. If they can buy a certain amount of things with $1000 today, people want to be able to buy at least the same things in the future with their savings. Discuss the following.

a. If you saved $1000 today to buy a $1000 computer next year, would you be able to buy it if your savings earned 5% and the price of the computer stayed the same? (*Yes because you'd have approximately $1050 to buy the $1000 computer.*)

b. If you saved $1000 today to buy a $1000 computer next year, would you be able to buy it if your savings earned 5% and the price of the computer increased 3%? (*Yes because you'd have approximately $1050 to buy the computer that would cost $1030.*)

c. If you saved $1000 today to buy a $1000 computer next year, would you be able to buy it if you savings earned 5% and the price of the computer increased 7%? (*No because you'd have approximately $1050 to buy the computer that would cost $1070.*)

6. Summarize by pointing out that inflation reduces the purchasing power of accumulated savings. If people's savings are going to have the same purchasing power in the future, then the interest/earnings on the savings must be equal to or greater than the inflation rate. For example, if the inflation rate is 4%, then the interest rate must be at least 4% so the saver could still be able to buy the same amount of things in the future with the money (principal).

7. Explain that this is exactly what the inflation-indexed I Bond is designed to do — protect the purchasing power of an individual's principal AND pay guaranteed earnings. The I Bond interest rate has two parts: a fixed interest rate that lasts for 30 years and an inflation rate that changes every six months if inflation changes. For example, an I Bond may pay a fixed interest rate of 4%. The semiannual inflation rate may be 2% for the first six months and 2.5% for the second half of the year. Therefore the combined interest rate would be 4% + 2% + 2.5%.

8. Give each student a copy of Activity 1-5, and assign. Display Visual 1.7 to check answers.

Check It — Assessment

1. Divide the students into small groups. Assign each group a different savings instrument. For example, money market funds, treasury bonds, treasury bills, savings accounts, and certificates of deposits. Ask students to do some research to answer the following questions.

    a. What is this savings instrument called?
    b. Does it require a minimum balance?
    c. Are there fees or penalties if you withdraw your money before a specified time?
    d. Is this savings method more or less risky than savings bonds?
    e. What is the interest rate on this savings instrument?
    f. Is interest compounded annually, semi-annually, quarterly, daily?
    g. How is the purchasing power of the savings protected from inflation?

2. Tell students that each group must prepare a brief presentation in which they compare the advantages and disadvantages of the savings instrument they choose with the advantages and disadvantages of an I Bond.

Saving is income not spent now. The accumulated amount of money saved over a period of time is called savings. Suppose there are 180 days in a school year, and you begin saving $2.00 each day in your bank beginning in the 7th grade. You save all the money each year. Your bank fills up and you start saving in an old sock. Answer the following questions.

1. Calculate the amount of savings that you have at the end of each year. Please show your work on the back of this sheet. Record your answers for each year in the "SAVINGS" column of the table below.

GRADE LEVEL	SAVINGS
7th grade	
8th grade	
9th grade	
10th grade	
11th grade	
12th grade	

2. What would you have to give up each day in order to save $2.00? What do we call the item you would give up?

3. Write a formula to represent the calculations that you made for each year.

4. According to the formula, what will happen if you increase B?

Suppose that on the first day of eighth grade you receive the following message from Uncle Mort. "I am proud that you've been saving. I will pay you 10% on the balance that you saved in the seventh grade and 10% on the balance of your saving at the end of each year." You have $360 in your bank. Answer the following questions.

1. Calculate how much money you will have at the end of each year. Show your work on the back of this page. Write your answers in the "SAVINGS" column in the table below.

GRADE LEVEL	SAVINGS
7th grade	
8th grade	
9th grade	
10th grade	
11th grade	
12th grade	

2. Write a formula to represent the amount of savings accumulated at the end of each year.

3. How do the amounts you've calculated compare to your previous savings calculations? Why?

1. Write the basic percent equation that you have used in this lesson to solve for the part of the whole. Use the variables a, b, and c, where a is the percent, b is the whole, and c is the part of the whole.

2. Read the following sentences. Write an appropriate formula to use to solve for the percent of allowance saved OR the amount saved.

   - Mary received her weekly allowance of $10.
   - Mary used two one-dollar bills and two quarters.
   - Mary spent one-fourth of her allowance.

3. Answer the following questions, using the information on the overhead projector.

   a. How much did the total amount of savings increase from seventh grade until graduation from high school?

   b. How much did the saver actually deposit in the account during the 6 years?

   c. Rewrite the percent equation from #1 to find the percent of the whole.

   d. Use the equation in (c) to find the percent of the total accumulated savings that savers deposited.

   e. What amount of the savings accumulated as a result of interest and compounding?

   f. What percent of the total accumulated savings is this amount?

   g. Approximately 16% of the total amount of the savings accumulated because of interest earned on savings, even though the account only earned 5% interest per year. Why did this happen?

   h. What would happen if the saver kept the money in the account for ten more years?

Confounding Compounding

Uncle Mort has taught you a lot about saving. Now he's encouraging you to open a savings account. He says that it's best to have interest compounded as often as possible. You still aren't too certain what compounded more than once a year means or how it is done. Uncle Mort sends you an e-mail message with the following example.

Suppose that a bank offers a 5% interest rate, compounded semi-annually. At the end of six months, the bank will multiply your balance by ½ the interest rate and add that amount to your account. So, if you have $180 in the bank after six months, the bank will add $4.50 to your account. Your new balance will be $184.50. At the end of the next six months, if you still have $184.50 in your account, the bank will add $4.61 to your account. Your new balance will be $189.11.

1. What decimal amount would you use to calculate quarterly interest?

2. Suppose that the bank pays a 5% interest rate, compounded quarterly. You deposit $360 at the beginning of each grade. Complete the following table to calculate the total savings you'll have at the end of each year. The first two rows are completed for you.

Grade Level	Deposit Plus Previous Balance	First Quarter Interest	Second Quarter Interest	Third Quarter Interest	Fourth Quarter Interest	Accumulated Savings
7th grade	$ 360.00	$4.50	$4.56	$4.61	$4.67	$ 378.34
8th grade	738.34	9.23	9.34	9.46	9.58	775.95
9th grade						
10th grade						
11th grade						
12th grade						

3. How many dollars were deposited during the six years? _____

4. How much interest was earned? _____

Money Math (Lesson 1)

Mary Andrews received a $100 I bond from her uncle for her birthday. He told Mary that he paid the face value of the bond. Mary asked what face value meant. Her uncle said that he paid the amount shown on the face of the bond.

> *A picture of Dr. Martin Luther King appears on the $100 inflation-indexed I Bond.*

He told her that the fixed interest rate on the bond is 3.6%. The current semiannual inflation rate paid on the bond is 1.9%, and economists predict that it will stay the same for the rest of the year. Interest is paid every month, but earnings are compounded semiannually.

Mary is very confused by all this jargon. All she wants to know is what the bond will be worth on her next birthday. Using what you have learned about semiannual compounding and I Bonds, help Mary determine the value of her bond at the end of one year.

Answer the following questions on a back of this handout.

1. What is the combined interest rate?

2. Use the combined interest rate to estimate how much interest Mary would earn that year.

3. For the first half of the year, how much interest will Mary earn from the fixed interest rate?

4. For the first half of the year, how much interest will Mary earn from the inflation rate?

5. How much will her bond be worth after six months?

6. For the last half of the year, how much interest will she earn from the fixed interest rate?

7. For the last half of the year, how much interest will Mary earn from the inflation rate?

8. How much will her bond be worth after the second six months?

9. Why does the interest earned exceed the amount you estimated in #2?

- The word percent means "per hundred."

- A percent is like a ratio because it compares a number to 100.

- A percent is a part of a whole.

- A number followed by a percent symbol (%) has a denominator of 100. This means that it is easy to write as a fraction or a decimal. For example, if you earned a 90% on your last test, you also earned 90/100 that is the same amount as the decimal .90.

To find the percent, we use the following equation.

$$a\% = c \div b \quad \text{and} \quad a\% \cdot b = c$$

where **a** is the percent,

b is the whole, and

c is the part of the whole.

✏ **What percent of the students' families thought that Mrs. Addle was correct?**

In this example, 25 is the whole and 20 is the part of the whole, so we know **b** and **c**. Now, we must solve for **a**.

$$a \div 100 = 20 \div 25$$

What percent of 25 is 20?

$$a\% \cdot 25 = 20$$
$$(a \div 100) \cdot 25 = 20$$
$$.25a = 20$$
$$a = 20 \div .25$$
$$a = 80\%$$

80% of the students learned that their families agreed with Mrs. Addle.

✏ **How can 80% be stated as a decimal?**

$$80\% = 80 \div 100 = .80 \quad or \quad 8 \div 10 = .8$$

✏ **What percent of the students failed to do their homework?**

- The whole is represented by 100%.
- The part of the whole that did the homework is 80%, so 20% didn't.
  or, $(a/100) \cdot 25 = 5$,
- so that $.25a = 5$,
- so that $a = 5 \div .25$,
- therefore, $a = 20$ or 20% of the students didn't complete the homework.

✏ **How can 20% be stated as a decimal?** (*by converting 20% to 20/100 or 2/10 which equals 0.2*)

Grade Level	Accumulated Savings
3rd grade	$ 360
4th grade	720
5th grade	1080
6th grade	1440
7th grade	1800
8th grade	2160
9th grade	2420
10th grade	2780
11th grade	3140
12th grade	3500

Millionaire Rule 1:

Grade Level	Accumulated Savings
7th grade	$ 720
8th grade	1440
9th grade	2160
10th grade	2880
11th grade	3600
12th grade	4320

Millionaire Rule 2:

Money Math (Lesson 1)

A	B	C	D	E
Year	Beginning Amount	Interest Rate (5%)	Annual Interest	End-of-Year Amount
7th grade	$ 360.00	0.05	$ 18.00	$ 378.00
8th grade	738.00	0.05	36.90	774.90
9th grade	1,134.90	0.05	56.75	1,191.65
10th grade	1,551.65	0.05	77.58	1,629.23
11th grade	1,989.23	0.05	99.46	2,088.69
12th grade	2,448.69	0.05	122.43	2,571.12

1. $a\% \cdot b = c$; a = percent; b = whole; c = part of whole

2. $25\% \cdot \$10 = \$2.50$

3a. $\$2,571.12 - \$360 = \$2,211.12$

3b. $\$360 \cdot 6 \text{ years} = \$2,160$

3c. $a\% = c \div b$

3d. $\$2,160/\$2571.12 = 84\%$

3e. $\$2,571.12 - \$2,160 = \$411.12$

3f. $\$411.12/\$2,571.12 = 16\%$

3g. The interest was compounded. The saver earned interest on both deposits and accumulated interest.

3h. The amount of savings would increase even more.

1. $0.05/4 = .0125$

2.

Grade	Deposit Plus Previous Balance	First Quarter Interest	Second Quarter Interest	Third Quarter Interest	Fourth Quarter Interest	Accumulated Savings
7th	$ 360.00	$4.50	$4.56	$4.61	$4.67	$378.34
8th	738.34	9.23	9.34	9.46	9.58	775.95
9th	1135.95	14.20	14.38	14.56	14.74	1193.83
10th	1553.83	19.42	19.66	19.91	20.16	1632.98
11th	1992.98	24.91	25.22	25.54	25.86	2094.51
12th	2454.51	30.68	31.06	31.45	31.84	2579.54

3. $2160.00

4. $419.54

1. $3.6\% + 1.9\% + 1.9\% = 7.4\%$

2. $\$3.60 + \$1.90 + \$1.90 = \$7.40$

3. $.036 \div 2 = .018;$ $\$100 \times .018 = \$1.80$

4. $\$100 \times .019 = \$1.90$

5. $\$100 + \$1.80 + \$1.90 = \$103.70$

6. $\$103.70 \times .018 = \$1.87$

7. $\$103.70 \times .019 = \$1.97$

8. $\$103.70 + \$1.87 + \$1.97 = \$107.54$

9. Because of compounding, Mary earns interest on her principal AND on the interest earned in the first half of the year.

Lesson Description	Students hear a story about Tom, a middle-school student who wants to redecorate his bedroom. They measure the classroom wall dimensions, draw a scale model, and incorporate measurements for windows and doors to determine the area that could be covered by wallpaper. Students then hear more about Tom's redecorating adventure, learning about expenses, budget constraints, and trade-offs. For assessment, students measure their rooms at home. This lesson requires that students know how to measure, or a review may be necessary before teaching.
Objectives	Students will be able to: 1. measure in feet and calculate square feet. 2. define area. 3. calculate the area of squares and rectangles. 4. define trade-offs, budget constraint, and expenses. 5. identify trade-offs.
Mathematics Concepts	measurement, dimension, height, width, length, area, average
Personal Finance Concepts	trade-offs, budget constraint, expenses
Materials Required	• a sign for each wall in the classroom (labeled A, B, C, and D) and masking tape (Prior to class, tape a letter sign to each wall in the classroom.) • a yardstick or steel tape measure and a sheet of paper for each group of students • one sheet of graph paper, one ruler, and one protractor for each student • transparency of Visual 2-1 • calculators (optional) • copy of Activity 2-1 for each student • book of wallpaper samples or allow students to visit Internet sites • 2-3 sheets of 8½" x 11" paper, scissors, crayons, markers, and/or colored pencils for each student • 9" x 12" piece of oak tag for each student • scissors and glue or glue sticks

Time Required	2 - 3 days

Procedure	**Get Ready**

1. Ask students if they're happy with the way their rooms at home are decorated. (*Answers will vary.*) Discuss the following.

    a. If you like your room, what do you like? (*color, wallpaper, furniture, posters, pictures*)
    b. If you don't like your room, what would you change? (*color, wallpaper, posters, pictures*) Why? (*paper is for younger kids, tired of the color or the wallpaper pattern, want posters and pictures related to new things*)

2. Explain that they will learn about a middle-school boy, Tom, who's unhappy with the way his room looks. Read the following story to the class.

    My room still looks EXACTLY the way it did when I was ten. Can you believe it? I just can't stand it any longer. So, over the weekend, I asked Mom if I could change my room. I told her that I wanted to rip down the race car wallpaper and put up something else. Mom said I could change my room, but I couldn't put up strange stuff like skull and crossbones wallpaper. She also said I would have to figure out how much wallpaper I needed before we could shop for wallpaper. I said, "That's easy, I need enough to cover all the walls. The person at the wallpaper store will know." Mom replied, "Tom, the person at the store needs some help. You have to measure the walls and have some idea about how much wallpaper you need before you ever go to the store. This is where all those important math skills you've learned at school will come in handy." Let's talk about what you need to know."

    Maybe this redecorating idea wasn't such a great one after all. Maybe I can just stick some posters over the race cars.

3. Discuss the following.

    a. Do you think Tom should give up on the wallpaper idea? (*Answers will vary.*)

b. Have any of you ever helped someone in your family buy wallpaper? (*Answers will vary.*)

c. What math skills will Tom need to buy wallpaper? (*measurement skills, understanding of dimensions, addition, subtraction, multiplication, and division skills*)

d. If we wanted to buy wallpaper for the classroom, what dimensions would we need? (*the height and width of the walls*) Why? (*These measurements allow us to determine the amount of wall space to be covered with wallpaper.*)

e. What is a baseboard, and why do you measure only to the baseboard and not to the floor? (*A baseboard is a strip of plastic or wood that fits on top of the floor and along the bottom of the wall. The wallpaper will stop at the baseboard. It won't cover the baseboard.*)

4. Divide students into groups of 3 or 4, and distribute a yardstick or steel tape measure and a sheet of paper to each group. Draw the table below on the board, and ask a member of each group to draw the same table on the sheet of paper. Tell students to measure to the nearest quarter of an inch. Allow time for groups of students to measure the walls in the room and record the measurements.

Note: If there are large errors in measurement of any wall, have the groups measure again.

Wall	Height of Wall in Feet	Width of Wall in Feet
A		
B		
C		
D		

Get Going

1. Have each group report its measurements. As each reports, record the measurements in the table on the board as in the sample table below.

Wall	Heights of Wall in Feet	Widths of Wall in Feet
A	8', 8'6", 8'3", 7'9", 8'	10', 10'6", 10', 10'3", 10'3"

2. Point out any differences in measurements. Given differences, ask for a way to calculate a single height and width for each wall, given the data. Guide students to recognize that they can calculate an average height and width for each wall. Ask how to calculate the average height of the wall. (*Add all height measurements and divide by the number of groups.*) Allow time for students to compute the average heights. Then ask how to calculate the average width for each wall. (*Add all width measurements for each wall and divide by the number of groups.*) Have students compute the average widths.

3. Record averages on the board, and explain that when determining how much wallpaper to buy, experts recommend that people round to the next highest half foot or foot as needed. If necessary, round the averages calculated.

Graph It

1. Distribute rulers and graph paper. Have students draw a scale model of the room using the averages and a scale of 1" = 1'.

Students should notice they need measurements of doors, windows, chalkboards and other areas that wouldn't be covered with paper.

2. Have one group measure the windows, another measure the chalkboard, and another measure the doors, then record the measurements on the board. Tell students to use this information to complete the drawing.

Keep Going

1. Discuss the following.

   a. How can these measurements be used to determine the amount of wallpaper needed for the room? (*by determining the area of wall space that must be covered*)
   b. What is "area"? (*the measure of the interior region of a two-dimensional figure*)
   c. What type of figure is the wall? (*rectangle*)
   d. How do we determine the area of a rectangle? (*Answers will vary. Guide students to recall that they must multiply the length of the rectangle by the width.*)
   e. What is the length of the front wall of the classroom? (*Answer depends on the classroom.*)

f. What is the width of the front wall of the classroom? (*Answer depends on the classroom.*)

g. Using your drawing, how can you determine the area of the front wall? (*count the number of squares inside the rectangle*)

h. Why is area expressed in square units — in this case, square feet? (*It is the sum of the squares inside a two-dimensional figure.*)

i. Multiplying height by width, how can you determine the total wall area in the room? (*Multiply the height of each wall by the width of each wall and add the four products.*)

2. Have students think of another way to do this problem that might take less time. Guide them to recognize that they could first add the width of all four walls and then multiply that sum by the height of the four walls. Have them calculate in this way and compare answers. Of course, the answers will be the same.

3. Ask if they still have a problem to solve before they could purchase wallpaper.

a. What is it? (*The measurement includes the doors, windows, and chalkboards that shouldn't be covered with paper.*)

b. How can the measurements be corrected? (*by subtracting the area of the doors, chalkboards, and windows from the total area*)

c. Point out that each single roll of wallpaper contains 30 square feet of paper. How can the number of single rolls of wallpaper to buy to paper the walls in the classroom be determined? (*divide the area of the wall space by 30*)

4. Read the following scenario to the class.

My mom and I figured out the wall area of my room. Then we went shopping at a huge hardware store. It had everything — wallpaper, paint, lamps, blinds, rugs, picture, and posters. I found some great wallpaper for only $36 per single roll!

I gave the store clerk the area that Mom and I calculated. She explained that I would need at least 15 single rolls of paper. I also found two posters, a basketball lamp, some great soccer posters, and paint for the baseboards in my room.

My room was going to look fabulous, but my mom spoiled the whole thing with, you guessed it, MATH! First she asked, "Tom, if the wallpaper is $36 a roll and you need 15 rolls, how much will that cost?" I replied, "Oh, Mom. I don't know. Don't you have a calculator?"

5. Pause and have students help Tom with this calculation. (15 x $36 = $540) Continue reading the story.

"Tom," my mom said anxiously, "that's $540 just for wallpaper. How much is the gallon of paint?" "Uh, $25," I answered. "And, you want pictures, posters, a lamp, a bedspread, and blinds?" I think you should know that there's a limit to what I will spend," Mom explained.

Well, that ended my shopping spree. My mom told me that she was willing to spend a total of $700 on the project. She said that $700 was my budget constraint. How am I supposed to get everything I want? If I spend $540 for wallpaper, I'll only have, um . . . . Does anyone have a calculator?

6. Pause and have someone help Tom with the calculation. *($700 - $540 = $160)*

7. Explain that Tom has a budget constraint of $700. A **budget constraint** is a limit to the amount that may be spent. Because of this constraint, Tom can't have everything he wants. He must limit his expenses to $700 or less. Explain that **expenses** are payments for goods and services.

8. Explain that Tom must make some choices. His mom suggested that first he should make a list of the expenses for his room. Display Visual 2-1 and explain that this is Tom's list. Discuss the following.

a. How much more are Tom's expected expenses than his budget constraint? (*$935 - $700 = $235*)

b. Suggest some changes that Tom might make. (*only buy one lava lamp, only buy one soccer poster and frame, wait and ask for the black light and black light poster as a holiday gift, eliminate the basketball hoop*)

9. Point out that Tom must make some trade-offs. **Trade-offs** involve giving up some of one thing to get more of something else. If Tom buys more expensive wallpaper, he must give up some of the other things that he wants. Continue the story.

"Look, Mom," Tom said in a reasonable voice, " I'm perfectly willing to give up the blinds and the bedspread. After all, our apartment is on the second floor, so I don't need blinds. I hate to make my bed, so why have a bedspread?"

Sounding exasperated, Mom responded, "Tom, we need blinds or curtains on the windows. That's one of the landlord's rules, and I want the apartment to look nice. You may not like making your bed; however, I like it when your bed is made, so the bedspread is a must. Do you have other suggestions?"

Tom replied, "I could buy one lava lamp instead of two and one soccer poster and frame instead of two. I could wait and ask for the black light and black light poster for a holiday or birthday gift. I could do the same with the basketball hoop. I guess I have to have a trash can, right?" Tom's mother nodded. "Well then, that's all I can think of."

"Okay, Tom, how much would you save if you did all that?" Tom's mom asked.

"Gosh, Mom, are you sure you didn't bring a calculator?"

10. Pause and ask how much Tom would save with all those changes. (*$22.50 by eliminating a lava lamp, $37.50 by eliminating one soccer poster and frame, $15 by eliminating the basketball hoop, and $30 by eliminating the black light and black light poster for a total of $105*) Discuss the following.

a. At first, what trade-off is Tom willing to make? (*He is willing to give up the bedspread and blinds in order to have the wallpaper.*)

b. What does his mom think of this? (*She isn't willing to make the same trade-off.*)

11. Continue the story.

"Mom, I figured it out. If I make all the changes we discussed, I can save $105, but that still isn't enough. Maybe I should just stick with the race cars," Tom said dejectedly.

"Tom, I have a better idea. You know, you chose a designer wallpaper," she said.

"Yes, isn't it great? The designer's name is Tom, too," Tom said.

"Well, that's not such a good reason to buy the paper, and that wallpaper is much more expensive than some others. Plus, that paper has a large pattern repeat. That's why you must buy 15 rolls of paper. You need more paper in order to match the pattern as the paper is hung. It would be a good idea if you were a wiser buyer. There are many other books containing wallpaper samples. Some might be just as nice but cost less. Why don't you spend a little more time looking? Perhaps you should think carefully about what's really important to you. Is the designer wallpaper more important than the other things you want for your room?"

12. Ask why Tom's mom was right. (*Tom hadn't considered all available options.*) Explain that after Tom looked for a while, he found wallpaper for only $15 a single roll and the pattern repeat was smaller, so he only needed 14 rolls. He decided he would rather have the less expensive wallpaper in order to have more of the other items he wanted. Discuss the following.

a. What trade-off is Tom willing to make now? (*He's willing to give up the designer wallpaper in order to have the other items he wants for his room.*)

b. How much would the new wallpaper selection cost?
(*14 rolls x $15 = $210*)

13. Display Visual 2-1 again, explaining that Tom's expenses have changed. Ask for alternative approaches to calculating a new total. Write student approaches in sentences on the board. Then have students convert the sentences as mathematical statements, using symbols and parentheses as needed.

Subtract $540 from $935 and add $210 to the difference.

($935 - $540) + $210 = $605

Add all numbers substituting $210 for $540.

(45 + 25 + 75 + 15 + 210 + 100 + 90 + 10 + 20 +15) = $605

Subtract $210 from $540 and subtract the difference from $935.

$935 - ($540 - $210) = $605

Graph It

Using a computer or pencil, paper, protractor or ruler, have students create a bar or circle graph showing the portion of Tom's decorating budget represented by each expenditure.

Wrap It Up

Review lesson content with the following questions.

1. What is area? (*the measure, in square units, of the interior region of a two-dimensional figure*)

2. What's the formula for calculating the area of a rectangle?
($A = lw$)

3. Sue's parents told her that she could buy new clothes, but her budget constraint was $125. What does that mean? (*Sue must limit the amount that she spends to $125 or less.*)

4. What is an expense? (*an amount spent to purchase goods or services*) Give an example of an expense you had this week. (*lunch, video rental, candy*)

5. Trade-offs involve giving up a little of one thing in order to get a little more of something else. If your parents said that you could have $5 more allowance a week for watching your younger brother after school on Fridays for one hour, what trade-off are they asking you to make? (*give up one hour of free time on Fridays in order to have $5 extra to spend/save*)

Check It — Assessment

1. Have students draw a scale model of their bedroom or another room in their homes, using graph paper and a ruler. The scale should be 1" = 1'. The model should illustrate walls, doors, and windows. Using the scale model, students should determine the amount of wallpaper needed to paper the room.

2. Distribute Activity 2-1 to each student, review instructions, and have students complete the worksheet.

Going Beyond — A Challenge Activity

Have students visit the following web sites to see examples of: drop match, straight-across match, and random match.

- *www.paperhanging.com/ class/patterns.html*
- *www.pdra.org/FAQs/ wallcoverings/#Q08*

As an alternative, bring in a book of sample wallpaper so students can look at different types of pattern repeats.

1. Ask what a pattern repeat is. After a few answers, explain that on most wallpaper, there is something called a pattern repeat. This is the vertical distance between one point on a pattern design to the identical point vertically. This pattern repeat is an integral part of the design. If the pattern repeat is large, the consumer must buy extra paper to match the pattern. If the pattern is random or the repeat pattern is small, the consumer won't need to buy as much extra paper.

2. Tell students that they will design their own wallpaper. The paper must have a straight-across or a drop-match pattern. They must design enough paper so that another student can cut the paper into strips and cover a 9" x 12" area with it.

3. Distribute 2-3 sheets of 8½" x 11" paper, crayons, scissors, markers, and colored pencils. Tell students to draw patterns, using a landscape orientation. Have them carefully cut the sheets into 2¾" x 8½" strips. When finished, have students trade designs. Give each student a piece of 9" x 12" oak tag (or an 8½" x 11" sheet of paper) and a glue stick or glue. Tell them to match the strips as though they were hanging paper by gluing the strips on the oak tag with a portrait orientation.

Read the paragraphs below and answer the questions that follow.

Kristen wants to buy a new video game with a price of $65. Kristen receives $15 for an allowance each week. She has been trying to save $5 each week for the last 5 weeks. So far, she has $5. Kristen is very frustrated. She can't figure out what she is doing wrong.

She must use her allowance for school lunches as well as for any entertainment or activities during the week. Last week Kristen paid $1.50 each school day for lunch. Kristen's neighbor said that he would pay Kristen $10 to rake leaves on Saturday afternoon, but Kristen wanted to go to the movies with her friends. The ticket for the matinee was $4.00, and she spent another $2.50 on popcorn and soda. While she and her friends waited for their ride home, she spent $1.00 playing video games at the arcade in the theater.

1. What are expenses? In the space below, write a list of Kristen's expenses for last week.

2. Kristen chose to go to the movies with her friends rather than rake leaves. She gave up earning some extra money to spend more time with her friends. What is this called?

   _____

3. Recommend some simple changes Kristen could make to save more of her allowance.

   _____

   _____

4. Kristen and her family are going on vacation. Her mother told her that she could spend $30 on souvenirs, video games, and miniature golf during the week. What is Kristen's budget constraint for the trip?

   _____

Tom's Expenses

2 lava lamps	$ 45
one gallon of high-quality paint	25
2 soccer posters with frames	75
over-the-door basketball hoop	15
15 single rolls of wallpaper	540
bedspread	100
2 blinds for windows	90
one black light poster	10
one black light	20
black-light trash can	15
TOTAL	$ 935

Math and Taxes: A Pair to Count On

Lesson Description	Students examine careers and reflect on how workers use math in their occupations. They study selected occupations, learning about the work skills (human capital) that different workers possess and salaries that those workers earn. Next, students learn about how taxes are paid on income that people earn and how income tax is calculated. They learn how the progressive federal income tax is based on the ability-to-pay principle.
Objectives	Students will be able to: 1. describe examples of human capital. 2. explain the link between human capital and income earning potential and provide examples. 3. define and provide examples of human and capital resources. 4. define and provide examples of income, saving, taxes, gross income, and net income. 5. define and provide examples of ability-to-pay and progressive tax. 6. calculate tax rates (percents) and the dollar amount of taxes. 7. read and understand tax tables.
Mathematics Concepts	computation and application of percents and decimals, using and applying data in tables, reasoning and problem solving with multi-step problems
Personal Finance Concepts	income, saving, taxes, gross income, net income
Materials Required	• copy of Activity 3-1, cut apart so there is one card for each group of 3-4 students • calculators • copy of Activity 3-2, cut apart so there is one card for each pair of students • copy of Activity 3-3 for each pair of students • black markers, chalkboard, masking tape • copy of Activity 3-4 for each pair of students • copy of Activity 3-5 for each student • transparency of Activity 3-5 • copy of Activity 3-6 for each student • transparencies of Visuals 3-1 through 3-4

Time Required	3 - 4 days

Procedure	**Get Ready**

1. Divide the class into groups of 3 or 4. Give a card from Activity 3-1 to each group.

2. Explain that each card describes a person with a particular occupation and a problem facing that person. Tell students to read the cards, decide what types of math skills/calculations each person must use to solve his or her problem, solve the problem where possible, and explain their reasoning in words.

3. Allow time for students to work. Have groups share the information on their cards, the type of math skills required, and their answers and reasoning. Discuss the following.

   a. What did all people described on the cards have in common? (*They all used mathematics skills to solve a work-related problem.*)
   b. What types of mathematics skills were required? (*basic computation skills, calculation of area and volume, conversion from customary to metric measurement, understanding calculation of averages, calculation of percentages*)
   c. Think of other occupations that also require the use of mathematics skills. (*Answers will vary.*)
   d. Can you think of tasks that you or others at home do that require the use of mathematics? (*cooking, painting, wallpapering, buying carpeting, sewing, woodworking, doing math homework, balancing the checkbook*)

4. Divide students into pairs, and give a card from Activity 3-2 to each pair.

5. Tell students that these are occupation cards. Ask each pair to identify only the occupation to the class. Pairs should not read the information on the card to the class. After each pair states its occupation, discuss the following with the class.

a. What type of work does a person with this occupation do? *(Answers will vary.)*

b. What type of math skills do you think a person with this occupation might use? *(Answers will vary but might include: basic calculations, graphing, interpretation of data, charts, and tables, geometry, algebra.)*

6. If students have questions about a worker, attempt to answer the questions as a class.

7. Have each pair answer the questions on Activity 3-3 based on the occupation chosen. Tell each pair to write its occupation on the back of Activity 3-3 with a black marker. Tell each pair to tape the paper with the occupation to the chalkboard.

8. Have one member of each pair identify the occupation, describe the education necessary, and the math skills involved. After all occupations have been identified, discuss the following.

a. Which occupation do you think earns the highest salary? *(Answers will vary.)*

b. Which occupation do you think earns the lowest salary? *(Answers will vary.)*

9. Combine student pairs into small groups. Have groups consider the occupations on the board and rank them according to yearly wage. The first occupation they list should be the occupation they think earns the highest wage, the second occupation should be the one they think earns the next highest wage, and so on.

10. Allow time for students to work. Have a volunteer group place the signs on the board in order (left to right) according to its list. Allow time for other groups to comment or make changes.

11. Have a student who worked with a particular occupation go up to the board and write the annual salary calculated for that occupation under the sign. Tell groups to check how well they did in ranking the occupations according to wage. Rearrange the signs and rewrite salaries so they are in the correct order. Discuss the following.

a. In general, do the very high-earning occupations require more or less education than the very low-earning occupations? (*more*)

b. Give an example of this generalization. (*Doctors earn higher wages and require more education than roofers.*)

12. Explain that people who work in the economy are **human resources**. **Human capital** is the quality and quantity of skills, education, and talents a person has. When people attend classes, become apprentices, obtain graduate degrees, and receive on-the-job training, they are investing in or improving their human capital. Have students identify examples of investment in human capital made by the people about whom they read. (*finished high school; attended trade school, college, or university; practice; apprenticeships*)

13. Have students explain how, in general, investment in human capital helps a person succeed or "pays off." (*People who invest in their human capital tend to earn more income over time than those who don't.*) Ask students why participation in mathematics classes throughout a student's school career is considered an investment in human capital. (*Math skills are essential to day-to-day living as well as required for various occupations. Learning and improving math skills improves a person's human capital.*)

Keep It Going

1. Explain that the wage or salary that people earn for the work they do is called **income**. There are three things that people do with their income. They can save it, spend it, and pay taxes with it. Everyone must pay taxes, but it is up to each individual whether to spend all the money, save almost all the money or some other combination.

2. Explain that **saving** occurs when people do not spend all their income on goods and services right away. **Taxes** are required payments to government. Discuss the following.

a. What taxes do you pay or are you aware adults pay? *(sales tax, income tax, property tax)*

    b. On what items do you pay sales tax? (*Answers will vary; however, usually on items purchased such as books, toys, clothes, and food.*)

    c. For what do you think the money collected as sales tax is used? (*Answers will vary.*)

    d. To whom do people pay property tax? (*local government*)

    e. For what do you think property taxes are used? (*Answers will vary.*)

    f. To whom do people pay income tax? (*federal and state governments*)

    g. For what do you think federal income taxes are used? (*Answers will vary.*)

3. Explain that federal income taxes are used to provide goods and services for citizens of the United States and to support the operation of the federal government. Ask students for examples of goods and services that the federal government provides. (*interstate highways, bridges, defense, medical research, national weather service, college loan programs, welfare payments, food stamps, approval of new drugs through the FDA, testing of meat and other agricultural products, disaster relief*)

4. Point out that people usually learn about income tax when they get their first job and must pay income taxes. However, the class will have the opportunity to learn from a young woman named Hannah. Read the following.

It is March in Hannah's senior year of high school. She is going to college in the fall and has a scholarship that covers two-thirds of her tuition. Her parents have agreed to pay the remaining one-third of her tuition and her room and board. Hannah must pay for her books each semester and for her miscellaneous expenses such as pizza, movies, and other entertainment. Hannah has been looking for a job for several weeks and has finally found one. Let's listen while Hannah tells her mother about her new job.

"Mom! I did it! I found a job. I'll earn $7.50 per hour at Toys for You. The manager said I could work weekends until school is out. That will be about 12 hours a week. She said that I

could work at least 25 hours a week during the summer. Mom, I'll have almost $2000 before college starts in the fall. If I combine that with what I've already saved, I'll have more than enough money for school. Can you believe it? I start next week — that's spring break. The manager said to count on 25 hours."

"Hannah that's great. Be careful though, before you start counting your money you need to remember that you have to pay taxes."

"Yeah, yeah, I know. They gave me some forms to fill out. I have to take them back tomorrow when I start. What's the big deal about taxes? All I have to do is fill out some forms. No problem."

"Hannah, it is more than just forms. Toys for You will take money from your check each week. That money will be sent to the state and federal governments. So don't plan to receive as much money as you expected each week."

"Come on, Mom. No matter what happens, you always have to talk about the negative stuff. Just be happy I have a job and that I start tomorrow. Now, I have to figure out what to wear for my first day. Maybe I'll go buy a new pair of slacks. After all, I am going to have a lot of money!"

5.   Pause and ask what Hannah's mom was trying to tell her about taxes and her pay. (*Answers will vary. Perhaps some student will recognize that because taxes will be withheld, Hannah's take-home pay will be less than she expects.*) Continue with the story as follows.

"Mom, Mom, where are you?" Hannah shouted. "I have a really big problem."

"Hannah, for heaven's sake, what are you yelling about?" Mom replied.

"I just got my first paycheck from Toys for You. Mom, they didn't pay me as much as they said they would. I've been cheated."

"Calm down and let me see your paycheck and receipt," Mom replied.

6. Display Visual 3-1 and continue reading.

    "Hannah, they paid you what they said they would. You worked 30 hours last week and your gross income is $225."
    "But Mom, the check is only for $162. That's the gross part if you ask me. They cheated me out of $63."

    "Hannah, gross income means the total amount you earned before taxes are withheld. The $162 is your net income. That's the amount left after you pay taxes. Remember I tried to tell you about taxes. Gross income is the actual amount you earned before taxes were withheld."

    "Oh, yeah, those forms I filled out, right?"

    "Yes, you filled out forms so that Toys for You could withhold federal income tax, Social Security and Medicare/Medicaid tax, and state income tax. Look at your pay receipt."

7. Refer to the transparency, and ask the following questions.

    a. What is Hannah's gross income? *($225)*
    b. What is gross income? (*the amount earned before taxes are withheld*)
    c. How was this amount determined? (*by multiplying the number of hours Hannah worked by her hourly wage, $7.50 x 30*)
    d. How much did Hannah pay in Federal Income Tax? *($33.75)*
    e. What percent of Hannah's total earnings is that? *(15%)* How did you find the percent? [*($33.75 ÷ $225) x 100*]

8. Ask if students know what FICA is. (*Answers will vary.*) Explain that FICA stands for Federal Insurance Contribution Act. This is money withheld to support Social Security and Medicare/Medicaid programs. **Social Security** is a tax paid by

today's workers that is used today to pay benefits to retired and disabled workers and their dependents. **Medicare** is a health insurance program for the aged and certain disabled persons. **Medicaid** provides health and hospitalization benefits to people who have low incomes. Continue discussing the pay receipt as follows.

a. How much did Hannah pay in Social Security and Medicare/Medicaid tax? *($20.25)*
b. What percent of Hannah's total earnings is that? *(9%)*
c. How did you find that percent? *[($20.25 ÷ $225) x 100]*
d. How much did Hannah pay in state income tax? *($9)*
e. What percent of Hannah's total earnings is that? *(4%)* How did you find that percent? *[($9 ÷ $225) x 100]*
f. What is Hannah's net income? *($162)*
g. What is net income? *(the amount of earnings received after taxes are paid)*
h. What percent of her income did Hannah pay in taxes? *(28%)* How did you find that percent? *([($225-$162) ÷ $225] x 100)* or *(15% + 9% + 4% = 28%)*

9. Continue the story.

   "Well, Mom, this is ridiculous. I am just a kid. Why do I have to pay taxes? What do I get from the government? This just isn't fair. I shouldn't have to pay taxes."

   "Hannah, think. You get some goods and services from the government. Plus, you won't earn much income during the year, so you'll probably get a refund. This means that the state and federal government may give back part or all of the income tax you paid. The Social Security taxes won't be refunded."

10. Ask what types of goods and services Hannah might receive from the government. *(highways, bridges, defense, fire and police protection, national weather service, testing of meat and other agricultural and medical products for her protection)*

11. Display Visual 3-2. Have students determine Hannah's expected earnings if she works 20 hours per week for 20 weeks. *($3,000)* Using this income and the tax table, show

Money Math (Lesson 3)

In these examples, gross income is equated with taxable income for simplification. We have suggested incorporating more advanced tax concepts in Going Beyond — A Challenge Activity, which is the extension section of the lesson.

how to look up the amount of federal tax that Hannah must pay.

- Find $3,000 of taxable income. Point to the next to last row.
- Explain that Hannah earned at least $3,000 but less than $3,050.
- Hannah is single. Read across the row to the column labeled "single."
- The amount found in this row and column is the amount of federal income tax Hannah must pay — $454.

12. Have students return to work with their "occupation" partners. Give a copy of Activity 3-4 to each pair and a copy of Activity 3-5 to each student. Go over the example at the bottom of the Activity 3-5.

13. Demonstrate how to use the tax rate schedules for the Fixits. Display the transparency of Activity 3-5. Have students write their answers as you demonstrate.

- Locate the "married filing jointly" schedule.
- Locate the income category for the Fixits. (*Over $283,150*)
- Read the base tax for this income category. (*85,288.50*)
- Show the tax rate for the income amount over 283,150. (*39.6%*)
- Calculate the amount of tax. (*[(285,000-283,150) x .396] = 732.60 + 85,288.50 = 86,021.10*)

14. Have students enter the information for the mechanic in the table on Activity 3-4 and complete the remaining problems.

15. When students have completed the work, display Visual 3-3 and have students check their answers.

16. Refer students to both the tax rate schedule and the table they completed. Ask students if they can determine any relationship between the amount of tax paid and the amount of income earned? (*Those who earn more, pay more in taxes.*)

17. Explain that the federal income tax system is based on the **ability-to-pay** principle of taxation. This principle states that a tax is fair if those who earn different amounts of income pay

different amounts of taxes. The federal income tax is a **progressive tax** — those who earn more income pay a larger percent of their income in tax.

18. (Optional) Have students choose a career/occupation in which they are interested. Use the Internet to determine the average yearly income for this occupation. Use the 1999 tax rate schedule to determine the amount of tax that would be paid and the tax rate as a single person or married couple.

Wrap It Up

Discuss the major points of the lesson as follows.

1. What is income? (*money earned for the use of resources*)
2. What is saving? (*income not spent on goods and services now*)
3. What are taxes? (*required payments to government*)
4. What is gross income? (*the amount earned before taxes and other deductions are withheld*)
5. What is net income? (*the amount available after taxes and other deductions are withheld*)
6. What are human resources? (*people working in the economy*)
7. What is human capital? (*the quality of the education, skills, and talents people possess*)
8. How can people invest in their human capital? (*through education, training, practice*)
9. What is the relationship between income and human capital? (*people with more and better human capital tend to earn more income*)
10. What are some examples of investment in human capital related to mathematics? (*learning basic computation skills, learning to calculate percents, ratios, area, perimeter, learning to use the calculator efficiently*)
11. What is the ability-to-pay principle of taxation? (*People who are able to pay more should pay more taxes.*)
12. What is a progressive tax? (*a tax requiring those who earn more to pay a larger percentage of their income in tax and those who earn less to pay a smaller percentage of their income in tax*)

Check It — Assessment

Hand out Activity 3-6 and have students complete the work. Display Visual 3-4, and allow students to check their work.

Going Beyond — A Challenge Activity

1. Using their work from Activity 3-4, have students consider the following problem using the example of Pierre.

    Next year, Pierre moves to a fancier restaurant and gets a great big raise! Now, Pierre has his own television show on the Eat Well channel. He's still single and earning $165,000 a year. How does the amount of tax he pays change? (He will pay more taxes because he has a larger income AND because he will pay a higher tax rate as he moves to a higher income category.)

2. Point out that the chef has moved to a new income category. Explain that people would usually say that Pierre has reached a new "tax bracket." In the higher tax bracket, Pierre will pay a higher percentage of tax. However, he pays the higher percentage only on his additional earnings beyond $158,550. This is the case with each tax bracket (income category) change. Taxpayers only pay the higher tax rate on a portion of their earnings. This idea of paying a higher percentage of tax on additional or extra earnings over some amount is referred to as marginal tax rates.

3. Have students speculate as to what marginal means in this context. Explain that in economics **marginal** means the extra or additional of something. So **marginal tax rates** are the extra taxes paid on extra earnings.

4. Have students look at the initial incomes of Pierre and the Joneses. Tell them to calculate the percent of total income that Pierre and the Joneses paid in income tax. When work is completed, have students share their answers. (*30,429 ÷115,000 = 26.5%; 46,324.50 ÷175,000 = 26.5%*)

5. Have students conjecture why that percent is lower than the marginal tax rates of 31% and 36%, respectively. (*The taxpayers don't pay the marginal tax rates of 31% and 36% on all their income. They pay the marginal tax rates only on the income that exceeds the lowest income amount in their tax bracket. On the other income, they are paying lower rates.*)

6. Explain that when taxpayers complete their income tax forms, they are allowed to deduct certain items from their taxable earnings. For example, taxpayers may deduct the interest on mortgage payments and charitable donations. Ask students how deductions would affect the amount of tax a person pays. (*Deductions reduce the amount of tax a person pays because deductions are subtracted from the gross earning amount.*)

7. Have students visit the IRS website to research the types of things that are tax deductible. Then have them complete scenarios for their occupation that include number of family members, mortgage costs, and charitable donations. Then allow them to complete a tax form using a commercial software tax package.

8. Have a certified public accountant visit the class and discuss deductions, exemptions, and tax credits. Have students complete the scenarios for their occupation/ family to include the number of family members and deductions. Then have them complete a tax form using a commercial software tax package.

9. Have W-4 forms available and help students complete those forms.

10. For additional information about Social Security students can visit the Social Security Administration website at www.ssa.gov/kids.

Wanda Woodworker is a carpenter. She is putting a two-room addition on Mr. Smith's house. She must decide how many pieces of wood to order to begin framing the room. Each piece of wood will measure 2' X 4'. The rooms are 12' X 15' and 15' X 15'. The 2' x 4' pieces are spaced 15 inches apart. How many 2' x 4' pieces does she need? Explain your reasoning.

Paul Prentice is a painter. He owns Paul's Paints and Papers. Paul charges $20 per hour for painting plus the cost of the paint. He is painting the exterior of Sandy Beaches' house. He has determined that he will need 15 gallons of paint. The paint Sandy selected is $25 per gallon. Paul estimates that the job will take 24 hours. What is the estimate? Explain your reasoning.

Patrick Zabrocki is a student teacher. He is teaching a fifth-grade class a lesson on averages. He has decided to begin by calculating the average height of students in the class. What does he have to do? List the steps and explain your reasoning.

Andrea Sooter is a furniture salesperson at a large furniture store. She receives a monthly base salary of $1000 plus a ten-percent commission on her sales. Last weekend was Labor Day weekend. The furniture store had a sale. Andrea's sales for the weekend brought her monthly total to $45,000. Andrea wants to estimate her pay for the month. What is the estimate? Explain your reasoning.

Alan Pretzal is an attorney. He works with many different clients. He is required to bill each client's account according the amount of time he spends working on that client's legal problems. Mr. Pretzal charges $100 per hour. Yesterday, he spent thirty minutes on the ABC account; fifteen minutes on the phone with another client, Mr. Jones; three and one-half hours on the Clark Candy account; ten minutes on the phone with Alexis Borgmeyer; and 45 minutes on E-mail correspondence with Henry's Hardware. How much should Alan bill each account? Explain your reasoning.

Kathryn McCorkle is a chef. She has an excellent recipe for burritos. The recipe serves six people. Kathryn is catering a party and wants to expand the recipe to serve 100 people. What must Kathryn do to determine how much of each ingredient she needs? Explain your reasoning.

Dr. Harry Lessman is a family practitioner. A patient, Ms. Strep, has a sore throat for which the doctor must prescribe an antibiotic. The dose of antibiotic is 10 milligrams per kilogram of body weight. This dose should be taken twice per day for ten days. Ms. Strep weighs 135 pounds. What dose should Dr. Lessman prescribe? Explain your reasoning.

Martin Walsh owns a gasoline station. It is time for him to order gasoline. The volume of each tank is 10,000 gallons. He knows how wide the tank is, how tall it is, and how deep it is. He has measured the height of gasoline remaining in each of the three tanks. What must Martin do to determine how much gasoline to order to fill the tanks? Explain your reasoning.

Courtney Rosser is a seamstress. She is making drapes for the windows in Mrs. Plum's conservatory. The windows are 48" wide and 63" long. There are four windows. The material Mrs. Plum has selected comes in widths of 24". Drapes require two and one-half times the width of the window. How much material should Courtney buy? Explain your reasoning.

1. You are a **carpenter**. Before graduating from high school, you met with a counselor who asked you many questions. She helped you recognize that you were physically fit, had excellent manual dexterity, good mathematics skills, and enjoyed creating things. She asked you if you might be interested in pursuing a career as a carpenter. You agreed that this might be a career for you. Once you graduated from high school, you took classes at a carpenter trade school and participated in an apprenticeship program that lasted three years and included on-the-job training.

   You are able to work from blueprints, measuring, marking, and arranging materials. You check the accuracy of your work with levels, rules, plumb bobs, and framing squares. Your hourly wage is $18.50. Last year, there were two months during which you were unable to work because of inclement weather.

2. You are a **painter and paperhanger**. During the summers of your junior and senior years in high school, you worked for a master painter who was an independent contractor. You set up and cleaned up. While helping, you learned a lot by watching the painter work. After you graduated from high school, you spoke with the contractor about being an apprentice. The contractor agreed to hire you. You attended classes and worked as an apprentice for three years. Some of the classes were mathematics classes.

   As a painter and paperhanger you have to prepare surfaces for paint or paper, mix and apply paints, incorporate some decorating concepts, and use cost-estimating techniques. Your hourly wage is $16. You worked the full year last year because you were able to work inside during inclement weather.

3. You are a **roofer**. You chose this career because your family owns a roofing company and has been in the roofing business for years. You learned your skills by participating in a three-year apprenticeship program that combined on-the-job training and classroom work. In addition to math classes, you also took a course in mechanical drawing. It is important that you stay in good physical condition and have excellent balance. Roofing is strenuous, hot, and dirty work. The longer you have worked in the business the more involved in budgeting, cost-estimation, and time estimation you have become. Last year, you earned $15 per hour. You were out of work three months because of bad weather.

4. You are a **teacher**. When you graduated from high school, you decided to attend a state university and obtain a degree in education. When you obtained your degree, you had to pass a test in order to be certified as a teacher. You are certified to teach elementary school. To maintain your certification, you must attend professional development programs each year. Within two years from receiving your certification, you must begin work on your masters degree.

You teach fifth-grade. You have a minor in math so you teach all of the fifth-grade math classes. In exchange, your teaching partner teaches all of the fifth-grade social studies classes. In addition to teaching math, you use math skills to prepare bulletin board displays, prepare grades, and in many other ways. You work very hard to provide hands-on activities and math manipulatives so your students will enjoy and learn mathematics.

You have been teaching for 1½ years. Your salary last year was $24,390. You are in school for ten months. You have two months paid vacation. However, during that time, you must pursue educational opportunities that will help you obtain your masters degree.

5. You are a **lawyer**. After graduating from high school, you earned a bachelor of science degree in economics. After completing your undergraduate degree, you entered law school. This took an additional three years. When you finished law school, you had to pass the state bar exam, a test that determines whether lawyers are certified to practice law in a given state. You obtained certification in your state and three neighboring states. You specialize in real-estate law. You are a partner in a firm and, as a result, earn a yearly salary plus bonuses. Your bonuses are based on the percentage of work you bring to the firm. You must attend yearly courses and workshops to maintain your qualifications and to learn about recent developments in real-estate law.

In your work, you must be able to analyze and interpret tables of data, graphs, and charts. You also employ basic mathematics computation skills. Last year, your salary combined with bonuses averaged $15,000 per month.

6. **You are a chef.** In high school, you took business mathematics and business administration. After high school, you attended a special cooking school — a culinary institute. This included classroom instruction as well as two internships at restaurants. Then you began work as an apprentice chef in a restaurant. Over time, you developed the experience necessary to establish your own catering business. You also took some basic business courses at a local community college. Some important skills necessary in your work are the ability to supervise less-skilled workers, limit food costs by minimizing waste, accurately anticipating the amount of perishable supplies needed, and maintain day-to-day bookkeeping. You measure, mix, and cook ingredients according to recipes. You also develop specialties. You organize and plan menus for your clients. Last year you estimate that you earned $17.50 per hour and worked an average of 50 hours per week.

7. **You are a physician**, a Doctor of Medicine. You examine patients; order, perform, and interpret diagnostic tests; diagnose illnesses; and prescribe and administer treatment. Your specialty is pediatric cardiology. While in high school, you took many mathematics and advanced science courses. In college, you majored in pre-med. After earning your bachelors degree, you went to medical school for four years. After medical school you spent 7 years in internship and residency. You had to pass both the state medical exam and a special exam given by the American Board of Medical Specialists. Now you are in practice with other pediatric specialists.

As a partner in a medical practice you have office hours, hospital visits, in-office meetings, and must be on call to serve patients every other weekend. In general, you work 50 to 60 hours per week. Last year, your average monthly salary was $18,750. You are still paying back student loans for your many years of education. But you are grateful to have reached your goal.

8. You are a **mechanical engineer**. You apply the theories and principles of science and mathematics to solve technical problems. You design products and machinery to build those products. Engineering knowledge is applied to improving many things.

   You were always fascinated with how things work. Often you took things apart to see how they worked and then put them back together. In high school, you took all the mathematics and science classes offered. After high school, you attended a university that offered degrees in a number of engineering fields. It took four years to complete your degree. You went on to earn a masters degree in engineering. You are licensed as a professional engineer. To get this license, you had to work four years after finishing school and pass a special exam. To maintain your license, you must attend programs and courses each year. These courses help you maintain the technical knowledge you need to be successful. You enjoy your work because it is challenging. Last year, your hourly salary was $35.

9. You are an **automobile mechanic/service technician**. You inspect, maintain, and repair automobiles and light trucks, such as vans and pickups with gasoline engines. People who did this work in the past were called auto mechanics. Now, because of computerized shop equipment and electric components, they are increasingly called service technicians.

   You've always liked learning how things work and fixing things that didn't work. You had good reading, mathematics, communication, and analytical skills. After high school, you attended an intensive, two-year program that included classroom work as well as hands-on practice. Your classroom work included English, basic mathematics, and computers. After receiving your associate degree, you went to work for a large automobile dealership. Each year, the dealership sends you to a training center where you learn how to repair new car models and receive special training in the repair of things like fuel-injection systems or air conditioners. Last year, the dealership was extremely busy. You worked many hours of overtime. As a result, your weekly salary was $1000.

Money Math (Lesson 3)

10. You are a **registered nurse**. You help promote health, prevent disease, and help patients cope with illness. You provide direct patient care so you must observe, assess, and record symptoms, reactions, and progress. You assist physicians during treatments and examinations; administer medications; and assist patients with recovery. You supervise licensed practical nurses and aides on your floor.

You are a very caring and sympathetic person. You can direct others, follow precise orders and determine when assistance is needed. After graduating from high school, you attended a university that offered a four-year bachelor of science in nursing degree. Your training included classroom instruction and supervised clinical experience in hospitals and other health facilities. You took courses in anatomy, physiology, microbiology, chemistry, nutrition, psychology, and other behavioral sciences as well as nursing. Upon graduation, you went to work at the hospital. You take continuing education courses to advance your skills. Last year, you earned $4,208 per month.

11. You are a **certified public accountant**. You prepare, analyze, and verify financial documents in order to provide information to your clients. You provide accounting, auditing, tax and consulting services for your clients. Your clients include businesses, governments, nonprofit organizations, and individuals.

You have a bachelor's degree in accounting. While in college, you participated in an internship program at a public accounting firm. After graduating from college, you took the certified public accountant exam. This two-day exam was very difficult, but you passed. As a result, you have a license as a certified public accountant (CPA). In order to renew your license, you must attend continuing education classes each year. Last year, you earned $95,000.

12. You are a **retail salesperson**. You sell new and used automobiles. You help customers find the vehicle they are looking for and try to interest them in buying the auto. You describe the auto's features, demonstrate its use, and show various models and colors. You are able to explain the features of various models, the meaning of manufacturers' specifications, and the types of options and financing available. You fill out sales contracts and complete the paperwork necessary for various payment options.

You have always been able to communicate clearly and effectively. You have a real talent for persuasion. After finishing high school, you earned an associate degree in communication. Once you completed your degree, you went to work for a large automobile dealer. You participated in a dealer-training program and in manufacturer's training. This training provided information about the technical details of standard and optional equipment. Each year, you attend additional training regarding new models. You have been working for the same automobile dealership for several years. Last year you earned $15 per hour.

13. You are a **firefighter**. You are called on to put out fires, treat injuries, and provide other emergency functions. Firefighting requires organization and teamwork. Between alarms, you clean and maintain equipment, conduct practice drills and fire inspections, and participate in physical fitness activities. You are required to prepare written reports on fire incidents and review fire-science literature to keep up with technology and changing practices and policies.

After graduation from high school, you had to pass a written exam; tests of strength, physical stamina, coordination, and agility, and a medical examination that included drug screening. You were among those with the highest scores on all the tests. That is why you were selected for your job. After accepting the job, you participated in weeks of training at the department's fire academy. This included classroom instruction and practical training. Some topics you studied were firefighting techniques, fire prevention, hazardous materials control, and first aid. You learned how to use axes, fire extinguishers, chain saws, ladders, and other firefighting equipment. You continue to study and acquire advanced skills in various fire-related topics. Last year, you worked an average of 50 hours per week and earned $22 per hour.

_____

1.   What is your occupation?

2.   What kinds of tasks do people with this occupation do?

3.   How much and what type of education does your occupation require? (vocational training, community college, four-year college or university, advanced degrees)

4.   What types of mathematics does the occupation require?

5.   What is your weekly and monthly salary or wage? How did you determine your weekly and monthly salary or wage?

6.   What is your annual salary? How did you determine your annual salary?

7.   Is this an occupation you might consider for your future? Why?

Enter the answers for the mechanic from the calculations done in class on the table below. Use Activity 3-5 to answer the following questions. Please use a separate sheet of paper to show your work. Enter your answers in the table below.

1. Pierre Haricots, an executive chef at an exclusive restaurant in New York City, earns $115,00 per year. If his filing status is single, how much federal income tax must he pay? What is the tax rate on the amount over the base amount?

2. In the Jones family, both parents work. One is a successful stockbroker and the other is a chemical engineer. Their combined income is $175,000. Their filing status is married filing jointly. How much federal income tax must they pay? What is the tax rate on the amount over the base amount?

Occupation	Yearly Income	Filing Status	Amount of Tax	Tax Rate on Income over Base Income
Fixits				
Pierre				
Joneses				

Money Math (Lesson 3)

Use this schedule if your filing status is **Single**

If your income is: over—	But not over—	Your tax is:		of the amount over—
$ 0	25,750	---------	15%	$ 0
25,750	62,450	3,862.50	+ 28%	25,750
62,450	130,250	14,138.50	+ 31%	62,450
130,250	283,150	35,156.50	+ 36%	130,250
283,150	-------------	90,200.50	+ 39.6%	283,150

Use this schedule if your filing status is **Married filing jointly**

If your income is: over—	But not over—	Your tax is:		of the amount over—
$ 0	43,050	---------	15%	$ 0
43,050	104,050	6,457.50	+ 28%	43,050
104,050	158,550	23,537.50	+ 31%	104,050
158,550	283,150	40,432.50	+ 36%	158,550
283,150	-------------	85,288.50	+ 39.6%	283,150

Tax calculation example for Mr. & Mrs. Fixit

Mr. Fixit is Cartown's best auto mechanic. He owns a busy auto repair shop and has a popular television show. He earns $285,000 a year. His wife doesn't work outside the home. Their filing status is married filing jointly.

1. Look at the bottom schedule because the Fixits are married filing jointly.

2. Under which income category do they fall? _____

3. What is the base (bottom) tax for this category? _____

4. What is the tax rate for any income above the lowest income amount in their category? _____

5. Calculate the total tax by adding the base (bottom) tax amount to the dollar amount of the percent of income over the lowest income.

6. What is the tax rate that the Fixits pay on all income? _____

Assessment—A Taxing Situation

This summer, you found your first part-time job working at the mall in the food court. You are earning $6.50 per hour and have been working 20 hours per week. You are paid every two weeks. You did some research and found out that the company will withhold 15% of your pay in federal income tax, 9% in FICA and Medicare tax, and 3% in state income tax. On a separate sheet of paper, answer questions 1-5. Be sure to show your work.

1. What is your gross income for two weeks?

2. How much do you pay in federal income tax each time you are paid? FICA? State income tax?

3. What is your net income each pay period?

4. At the end of 8 weeks, how much net income will you earn? How much federal income tax will you pay?

5. What human capital do you possess now? What investments can you make in your human capital?

6. Ms. Lawes is an attorney with a large, successful law firm. Last year she earned $135,000. How much tax must Ms. Lawes pay? Use the tax information below to answer the question.

If your income is over—	But not over—	Your tax is:	of the amount over—
104,050	158,550	23,537.50 + 31%	$104,050

7. Ms. Lawes' assistant earns $35,800 per year. Based on what you know about the federal income tax system, would you expect the assistant to pay a larger percentage of her income in tax than Ms. Lawes? Why?

Toys for You Pay Receipt Store #87				Hannah Smith SSN 494-90-1234	
Earnings	**Hours**	**Amount**	**Deduction**	**Current**	**Year To Date**
Regular	30.00	225.00	FICA Tax and Medicare Tax	20.25	20.25
Overtime	0.00	0.00	Federal Tax	33.75	33.75
Total	30.00	225.00	State Tax	9.00	9.00
Year-to-Date Gross		225.00	Total	63.00	63.00
			Net Pay	162.00	162.00

If your taxable income is —		And you are —			
At least	But less than	Single	Married Filing Jointly	Married Filing Separately	Head of Household
		Your tax is —			
2,975	3,000	448	448	448	448
3,000	3,050	454	454	454	454
3,050	3,100	461	461	461	461

Money Math (Lesson 3)

Occupation	Yearly Income	Filing Status	Amount of Tax	Tax Rate on Income over the Base Income
Pierre	$115,000	single	$30,429.00	31%
Joneses	$175,000	married filing jointly	$46,354.50	36%

Pierre: [.31 x (115,000-62,450)] + 14,138.50 = 30,429.00

Joneses: [.36 x (175,000-158,550] + 40,432.50 = 46,354.50

1. 6.50 x 40 = $260

2. federal income tax: $260 x .15 = $39

    FICA/Medicare: $260 x .09 = $23.40

    state income tax: $260 x .03 = $ 7.80

3. $260 – $39 - $23.40 - $7.80 = $189.80

4. $189.80 x 8 = $1518.40

    $39 x 8 = $312.00

5. Ability to read, use math skills, special talents students may possess
    Attend school. Finish high school. Go to college. Attend a trade school.
    Participate in an apprenticeship program.

6. [(135,000-104,050) x .31] + 23,537.50 = $33,132

7. No, because the federal income tax is designed to be a progressive tax. This
    means that those who earn less pay a smaller percentage of their income in
    tax than those who earn more.

Lesson Description	Students develop a budget for a college student using a spreadsheet. They examine the student's fixed, variable, and periodic expenses and revise to adjust for cash flow problems that appear on the first spreadsheet. Note: Instructions for using a spreadsheet are based on Microsoft ® Excel 97 but generally apply to other software such as Lotus 1-2-3©. This lesson is designed to increase student awareness and appreciation of the efficiency of using computer technology in math applications. The use of a computer lab is recommended. If the lesson is taught with a few computers, increase the time required indicated below.
Objectives	Students will be able to: 1. develop, analyze and revise a budget. 2. define and give examples of fixed expenses. 3. define and give examples of variable expenses. 4. explain how periodic expenses affect the budgeting process. 5. explain and give an example of a budget surplus and a budget deficit. 6. create a spreadsheet for a budget.
Mathematics Concepts	organizing numerical data, spreadsheet application, problem solving
Personal Finance Concepts	budget, gross and net income, payroll taxes, fixed expenses, variable expenses, periodic expenses
Materials Required	• computers with spreadsheet software • copies of Activities 4-1 through 4-6 • transparencies of Visuals 4-1 through 4-6
Time Required	2-4 days
Procedure	**Get Ready** 1. Give a copy of Activity 4-1 to each student, and read the scenario together. 2. Explain the main features of a spreadsheet, using the example. Have students complete the spreadsheet using the instructions provided. Note: if your spreadsheet program uses different

methods for formulas, explain them as students progress through the steps.

3. When students are finished, display a copy of Visual 4-1, so students may check their work. Debrief with the following questions.

    a. What is a budget? (*a plan of future income and expenses*)
    b. Why did Janna's parents tell her to make a budget? (*They wanted her to consider all income and expenses to make a careful decision about moving into an apartment.*)
    c. What are fixed expenses? (*expenses that are the same every month*) Give some examples of fixed expenses. (*monthly rent, car payment*)
    d. What are variable expenses? (*expenses that can vary from month to month*) Give some examples. (*food, clothing, entertainment*)
    e. The table indicates that Janna has a surplus. Why does she have a budget surplus? (*She has more income than expenses.*)
    f. Name some ways that Janna may be wrong about really having a budget surplus. (*Her income may be lower, and/or her expenses may be greater than indicated.*)

Keep It Going

1. Give a copy of Activity 4-2 to each student, and read the scenario together.

2. When students are finished, display Visual 4-2 (or hand out copies if the print is too small to be seen), so students may check their work. Debrief with the following questions.

    a. What's the difference between gross income and net income? (*Gross income is the total income that a person receives. Net income is gross income minus deductions.*)
    b. What payroll deductions did Janna have? (*federal and state income taxes as well as FICA*) Explain that people may have many more payroll deductions for things such as medical insurance or gifts to charitable organizations. Janna only has taxes removed from her paycheck.
    c. What is another name for net income? (*take-home pay*)

3. Give a copy of Activity 4-3 to each student, and read the scenario together.

4. When students are finished, display Visual 4-3 (or hand out copies if the print is too small to be seen), so students may check their work. Debrief with the following questions.

    a. Why do you think that car insurance payments were labeled as "periodic expenses?" (*The payments only occur twice a year, not every month. They do not occur regularly such as every week or month. They are payments that are made periodically, not regularly.*)

    b. According to your spreadsheet, what is the problem with a periodic expense? (*It makes the expenses higher in some months than others. In this case, the car insurance payments resulted in a negative surplus.*) Explain that a negative surplus is called a **deficit**.

    c. What could Janna do to resolve her problem? (*Answers will vary, but students are likely to point out that she could save some every month so she would have the money when she needed it.*)

5. Give a copy of Activity 4-4 to each student, and read the scenario in Part I together. Have students revise their budget spreadsheets once more. When they're finished, display Visual 4-4 (or hand out copies if the print is too small to be seen), so students may check their work. Debrief with the following questions.

    a. On Janna's spreadsheet, where does she have a problem? (*In the months of November and May, she has a large negative surplus.*)

    b. What is another term for negative surplus? (*deficit*)

    c. How did you spread out her car payments? (*by setting some aside every month*)

    d. Why does Janna still have a problem? (*She has a negative surplus every month.*)

    e. What recommendations could you make to Janna? (*Janna must either increase her monthly income or reduce her monthly expenses.*)

6. Assign Part II. When students are finished, have them report how they reduced Janna's expenses and why they chose that approach to her budget problem.

Wrap It Up

Review the main points of the lesson with the following questions.

1. What is a budget? (*a plan of future income and expenses*)
2. What are fixed expenses? (*expenses that are the same every month*)
3. Give some common examples of fixed expenses for a family. (*monthly rent, car payment*)
4. What are variable expenses? (*expenses that can vary from month to month*)
5. Give some common examples of variable expenses for a family. (*food, clothing, entertainment*)
6. What are periodic expenses? (*expenses that are made periodically, not regularly*)
7. Give some common examples of variable expenses for a family. (*car insurance, property taxes*)
8. What is a budget surplus? (*A budget surplus occurs when income is greater than expenses.*)
9. What is a budget deficit? (*A budget deficit is a negative surplus; it occurs when expenses are greater than income.*)
10. How can a budget help individuals and families? (*A budget helps people examine income and plan expenses carefully so that the budget is balanced or has a surplus. It helps people prepare for the future.*)
11. How does the use of a spreadsheet help people prepare budgets? (*A budget spreadsheet makes the preparation easier and faster. It helps people develop different income and expense scenarios and make adjustments to prepare for the future.*)

Check It — Assessment

Give a copy of Activity 4-5 to each student. Have students read the scenario and complete the work. (*See Visual 4-5 for final spreadsheet and Visual 4-6 for a suggested written response.*)

Going Beyond — A Challenge Activity

Give a copy of Activity 4-6 to each student, and read the scenario. Have students revise their budget spreadsheets a final time. When finished, have students explain how their budgets changed and what Janna had to give up to take the trip.

Janna is a college sophomore. Next year, she and three friends want to live in an apartment instead of the dormitory. She went home for the weekend to convince her parents about this good idea. Friday night, Janna announced, "The university will increase fees for room and board next year from $3,600 to $4,050. What a rip-off! That's $50 more each month, and it's not worth it. The dormitory is noisy at night when I study — a real distraction. The food in the cafeteria is barely edible, and it's not healthy food. Fifty girls share the same bathroom, and it's always dirty. People are really noisy."

Now, Janna was sure she had her parents' attention, so she continued her story. Heather, Amy, Lisa, and I found a furnished apartment close to campus with two bedrooms, living room, two baths, eat-in kitchen, and lots of parking. I'll pay one-fourth of the rent — $350 each month, including rent, electricity, water, sewer, and trash pick-up.

Then Janna explained that she would earn $325 per month as a part-time lab assistant in the chemistry lab, and her parents could give her $400 each month. That's the amount they paid for room and board at the university. She has a scholarship for her tuition and books. She pointed out that would leave plenty of money for other expenses.

Janna's parents agreed that everything she said was quite true, except for one thing. They didn't agree that she would have "plenty of money" left over for other expenses. They asked Janna to prepare a budget using the spreadsheet program on the computer. They said that she needed to think about every little aspect of her school life. She had included rent, which is a **fixed expense** — an expense that is the same every month. She hadn't included any **variable expenses** — expenses that may vary each month, such as groceries to replace the dorm meals and personal items. Janna went to the computer and prepared the following budget for her school year.

	A	B	C	D	E	F	G	H	I	J
	ITEM	SEP	OCT	NOV	DEC	JAN	FEB	MAR	APR	MAY
1										
2	*INCOME ITEMS*									
3	allowance	400.00								
4	part-time work	325.00								
5	**INCOME**									
6										
7	*FIXED EXPENSE ITEMS*									
8	Rent	350.00								
9	**FIXED EXPENSES**									
10										
11	*VARIABLE EXPENSE ITEMS*									
12	groceries/personal items	216.50								
13	**VARIABLE EXPENSES**									
14										
15	**TOTAL EXPENSES**									
16										
17	**SURPLUS**									

Money Math (Lesson 4)

What Is a Spreadsheet?

A spreadsheet organizes information into a table of horizontal rows and vertical columns. Each row has a number assigned to it, and each column has a letter assigned to it. Each box in the table is a **cell** in which data (information) are placed. The data may be numbers or letters. A cell is the intersection of a row and column and has an "address" identifying its coordinates. The column heading at the top shows the column letters, and the row heading at the left shows the numbers. For example, "allowance" is located in cell A3 and "216.50" is located in cell B12. You can change cells by using the arrow keys or by clicking on a cell using the mouse.

Creating Janna's Budget Spreadsheet

A **budget** is a plan of future income and expenses. It helps people anticipate future problems and create ways to correct for them. Create Janna's budget spreadsheet.

Step 1

- Click in the A1 cell using the mouse or go to A1 using arrow keys. Cell A1 looks different than the others with a dark border. When you are using a specific cell, it is called the **active cell**. Type "ITEM" in A1. Hit Enter

- Make A1 the active cell and widen column A, so all information in the column fits. Click Format, click Column, click Width, type "30" and click OK. You may also put the cursor on the line between A and B in the column heading. You'll see an arrow indicator. Click and drag until the width is 30.

- Click on B in the column heading, hold the Shift key down, and use the right arrow to highlight columns B through J. Using the mouse, click on Format, click on Cells, and click on Number under Category. Make sure that you have 2 decimal places. Click OK.

- Enter all data. You can format the data in a cell using the toolbar by aligning the data in the center, right, or left, and by putting the data in boldface or italics. Look at Janna's budget and format as you enter information in the cells.

Step 2

- B5 should have Janna's total income. The number is a sum of B3 and B4. Don't do the addition in your head and enter it. Tell the program to add the numbers. Type =B3+B4 in cell B5, hit Enter, and the correct answer should appear.

- There's only one fixed expense, so enter that amount in B9. Do the same with variable expenses in B13. The sum of fixed and variable expenses is total expenses. In cell B15, type =B9+B13.

- The difference between income and total expenses is called the surplus. In cell B17, type =B5-B15.

Step 3

- Complete the spreadsheet by entering the remaining months. Because Janna has the **same** income and expenses each month, simply copy and paste the data into each month. Make B3 your active cell, hold down the shift button, and use the down arrow to highlight B3 through B17. Then copy the data. Go to C3 and paste the data. You may also go to C3, hold down the shift button, use the right arrow to highlight columns C through J, and then paste the data. This shows how a computer spreadsheet is so much easier than completing a handwritten, computed table!

- Save your file.

Janna took her budget to her parents. They were impressed with her spreadsheet skills and said, "Janna, you really did a great job setting up a budget on a spreadsheet! You must have learned a lot in your computer class at college." Janna pointed out that she had a monthly surplus, and she asked if she could rent the apartment. Her parents replied that she still had many things to consider. "Janna, you must pay taxes on the income you receive — 15% federal income tax, 4% state tax, and about 8% for FICA."

"What's FICA?" replied Janna. "It's for Social Security and Medicare," her mom explained. Janna said, "I'm not going to retire for a long time. I don't need to pay that now." Mom pointed out that the law requires that Janna pay her share of Social Security and Medicare. Janna got out her calculator and said, "Well, taxes reduce my income by $87.75, but my surplus is much more, so I'll be okay. May I call my friends and tell them the good news?"

Dad said, "Not quite yet. I don't think you've considered all your expenses. You will probably share a phone and the basic monthly service is $40 that you can share with your friends. You also spend about $25 a month on your long distance phone calls. In the university dorm, your room included access to the Internet and cable TV. In an apartment, you'd have to pay for those things. Internet access would cost about $20 a month, and cable TV would cost about $30 a month for basic service. You could divide those expenses among your friends."

Janna exclaimed, "That's not so bad. That's only $5 a month for Internet, $10 a month for a phone, $7.50 a month for cable TV when we share expenses. That's the great thing about sharing an apartment. You can share expenses. Of course, I don't think my friends will want to share my long distance bill from calling my sister at her university in Canada. Let's see another $25 and $22.50 gone. That still leaves a surplus. We're going to have such a great time in our. . . ."

"Just a minute, Janna," Dad said. Last year, you spent about $50 a month on gasoline, and you had a lot of school and entertainment expenses. According to your credit card statements, that was about $100 a month for notebooks, clothes, movies, and so on. You spent about $125 a month on eating out!"

"Wait a minute!" exclaimed Janna. "I work in the summer and save $3000 for spending money during the school year. I forgot to include that in my income. Every month, I can withdraw one-ninth of my savings so that I have extra income every month. I'm not worried. This is all going to work out yet. Just wait and see. I'll go back and revise my budget."

Money Math (Lesson 4)
© Copyright 2001 by The Curators of the University of Missouri, a public corporation
Reproduction is permitted and encouraged.

A New Budget

Look at the following spreadsheet. You must enter some new categories (that is, rows). Now, Janna has another income source, some income deductions, and several new expenses.

	A	B	C	D	E	F	G	H	I	J
1	ITEM	SEP	OCT	NOV	DEC	JAN	FEB	MAR	APR	MAY
2	INCOME ITEMS									
3	allowance	400.00	400.00	400.00	400.00	400.00	400.00	400.00	400.00	400.00
4	Part-time work	325.00	325.00	325.00	325.00	325.00	325.00	325.00	325.00	325.00
5	savings withdrawal									
6	INCOME									
7										
8	DEDUCTIONS									
9	federal income tax (15%)									
10	state income tax (4%)									
11	FICA (8%)									
12	TOTAL DEDUCTIONS									
13										
14	NET INCOME									
15										
16	FIXED EXPENSE ITEMS									
17	Rent	350.00								
18	basic phone service									
19	cable television									
20	Internet access									
21	FIXED EXPENSES									
22										
23	VARIABLE EXPENSE ITEMS									
24	groceries/personal items	216.50								
25	Long distance phone calls									
26	eating out									
27	gasoline									
28	school/entertainment									
29	VARIABLE EXPENSES									
30										
31	TOTAL EXPENSES									
32										
33	SURPLUS									

NOTE: You now have more than one fixed and variable expense, so you must tell the computer to add the expenses. Go to B21 (which probably says 350.00). Type =B17+B18+B19+B20. Be sure to put a similar equation in B29 for variable expenses. Copy B21 to C21 through J21. Then use the same process for copying B29.

Janna rushed back to her parents after she worked hard on her budget spreadsheet. "Look!" she cried, "I did it! I still have a monthly surplus. Now, may I call Heather, Amy, and Lisa with the good news?"

The look on her father's face told her that the call would not take place. Dad looked at the spreadsheet, and once again told Janna what a terrific job she had done. "Janna, I'm proud of your good work. However, there's still something that you haven't considered."

"How could there possibly be anything else?" asked Janna. "This is a total picture of my financial life!"

"Not quite," replied Janna's father. "You forgot that you pay car insurance twice a year — $600 each time. That was the deal we made last year when we agreed that you could take your car to college. You must pay your car insurance on the first of November and again on the first of May."

"Okay, okay. I'll put that in my spreadsheet. I'll be right back." Janna was gone for a while, then came running back to her parents. "Just look at this spreadsheet! I've got a terrible problem! What am I going to do?"

Revise Janna's budget one more time.

- Periodic expenses occur occasionally, such as every six months or once a year.
- Go to cell A31, and insert four rows. Leave row 30 blank. Type *PERIODIC EXPENSES* (left alignment) in row 31. Type car insurance (left alignment) in row 32. Type PERIODIC EXPENSES IN ROW 33 (right alignment). Row 34 should be blank. See the following example.

	A	B	C	D	E	F	G	H	I	J
1	ITEM	SEP	OCT	NOV	DEC	JAN	FEB	MAR	APR	MAY
29	VARIABLE EXPENSES	516.50	516.50	516.50	516.50	516.50	516.50	516.50	516.50	516.50
30										
31	*PERIODIC EXPENSE ITEMS*									
32	car insurance									
33	PERIODIC EXPENSES									
34										
35	**TOTAL EXPENSES**									

- Enter car insurance payments in November and May. Enter a sum for periodic expenses in row 36.
- Go to B35 and revise the formula to include periodic expenses. Copy to the remaining cells in row 35. The surplus amounts in row 37 should change automatically.
- Save your file.

"What's the matter?" asked Janna's mother.

"Mom, I've got a terrible problem in November and May when I pay my car insurance. I don't want to choose between an apartment and my car!" exclaimed Janna.

Janna's mom told Janna to calm down. "Janna, she said. It's not as bad as it appears. You have a surplus of -518.42. That's a negative surplus or a deficit. Let's think about a solution to your problem."

Eventually Janna thought that she could save $100 each month so that she could pay for the car insurance when it was due. Mom thought that she had a great idea and told Janna to revise her budget one more time.

Janna said, "Boy, I'm glad that I learned how to use a spreadsheet. I would have to keep doing the WHOLE budget over and over again if I were doing this with paper and pencil. Thank goodness for computers!"

After a while, Janna reappeared. "I can't believe it! I've still got a problem! What's next? Now I have a negative surplus every month!"

Revise Janna's spreadsheet one more time to see what she's talking about.

- Janna has $1200 in car expenses. Insert a row above FIXED EXPENSES and under Internet access for "saving." Janna should save every month for car insurance, based on 9 months.
- In November and May, Janna's savings withdrawals will be $600 more than usual so she can pay her car insurance.
- Janna's deficit should be -51.75 every month.
- Save your file.

Part II

Just one more revision.

Make a decision for Janna so that she has a positive surplus once again. Janna really can't earn any more money. She's a full-time college student who already works as much as possible. As Janna said, "I guess that I'll just have to cut some expenses."

Enter your changes into the spreadsheet. Be prepared to explain and defend your changes to the class.

Help!

Read the following e-mail from Josh. Use the information to develop a spreadsheet budget for the school year. Determine if Josh has a budget surplus or deficit. Make sure to include a monthly payment for the money he owes you, his friend.

Write a response to Josh. In the message, explain what a budget spreadsheet is. Define budget deficit and budget surplus. Explain why Josh has one or the other. Also, define fixed, variable, and periodic expenses and make a list of Josh's fixed, variable, and periodic expenses. Suggest actions that Josh could take to bring his budget into balance.

Hi!

I thought I'd better write before my mother talks with yours. I had the money to repay what I borrowed from you. You know that I've been working all summer and saving for school clothes and the trip to *Three Banners over the Desert Water Park* at the end of May. I had plenty of money — enough to repay you and buy the other things. But that was before my life started to fall apart.

Luckily no one was hurt when the rock flew through Mrs. Smith's window. I could have earned more money to pay for the window if the blade on the lawn mower hadn't bent when it hit the rock. Oh, well, Mom says I won't have to pay to have the lawn mower repaired.

Anyway, I still have $270 left. Sometime during the year, I want to buy two pairs of Frumpy and Fitch jeans. They're $45 each. Admission to the water park along with food, video arcade, and shows will cost $72. It's worth it though. Mom says I have to put at least 10 percent of the $270 in my savings account. I'll never understand that. I put money in the account so I can buy stuff in the future. Who cares about that? I want stuff now. Mom also says that I have to provide my own spending money each month and money for gifts for holidays and birthdays. How am I supposed to know how much I'll need for things like that when they haven't even happened yet? I guess I'll need at least $10 every month for fun things like movies and skating. I'll also need at least $5 per month for food. How much do you think I'll need? How many months are there during the school year? You know what else? I promised to donate $2 each month to a Save the Rainforest fund at school. I decided that I just wouldn't do that because I've had all of these problems. Mom says a promise is a promise and I have to make the donation. Gosh, how would anyone know if I didn't? Parents! I guess I'll just buy the stuff I want right now. Then, I'll use the rest for spending money until I run out. But what about saving and the trip in May and the Rainforest fund? I give up!

I know I still owe you $25 and I'll repay you. Someday. Soon. I promise. You know you can trust me. I'm really reliable. It may take a while though. Hey, maybe I'll find a job shoveling snow in a few months.

Your friend,
Josh

Let's Work This Problem and Solve It!

Janna is very happy sharing an apartment with her three friends, and everything is working out fine. Janna developed a budget with a small surplus, and she's managed her money very well for two months. On October 31, Janna and her roommates had enough surplus to host a Halloween party.

While Janna was admiring Barbara and Claire's 60s costumes, Barbara exclaimed, "Have you heard about the trip to New Mexico for Habitat for Humanity®. It will happen during our spring break. I went last year, and it was such a wonderful experience. We repair and fix up homes for people who can't afford to do it themselves. There's a cost, but it's really worth it."

"How much?" asked Janna.

"Only $800, but you must pay a $200 deposit by the end of next week. Will you join us?" asked Claire.

"It sounds perfect. I worked with them last summer, and it was very rewarding. I'll work on my budget and let you know in a couple of days," replied Janna.

Using your last spreadsheet, work out a budget that will allow Janna to go on the trip. Be prepared to discuss how you changed the budget and what Janna must give up.

Budget Beginnings

	A	B	C	D	E	F	G	H	I	J
1	ITEM	SEP	OCT	NOV	DEC	JAN	FEB	MAR	APR	MAY
2	*INCOME ITEMS*									
3	allowance	400.00	400.00	400.00	400.00	400.00	400.00	400.00	400.00	400.00
4	part-time work	325.00	325.00	325.00	325.00	325.00	325.00	325.00	325.00	325.00
5	**INCOME**	725.00	725.00	725.00	725.00	725.00	725.00	725.00	725.00	725.00
6										
7	*FIXED EXPENSE ITEMS*									
8	rent	350.00	350.00	350.00	350.00	350.00	350.00	350.00	350.00	350.00
9	FIXED EXPENSES	350.00	350.00	350.00	350.00	350.00	350.00	350.00	350.00	350.00
10										
11	*VARIABLE EXPENSE ITEMS*									
12	groceries/personal items	216.50	216.50	216.50	216.50	216.50	216.50	216.50	216.50	216.50
13	VARIABLE EXPENSES	216.50	216.50	216.50	216.50	216.50	216.50	216.50	216.50	216.50
14										
15	**TOTAL EXPENSES**	566.50	566.50	566.50	566.50	566.50	566.50	566.50	566.50	566.50
16										
17	**SURPLUS**	158.50	158.50	158.50	158.50	158.50	158.50	158.50	158.50	158.50

	A	B	C	D	E	F	G	H	I	J
1	ITEM	SEP	OCT	NOV	DEC	JAN	FEB	MAR	APR	MAY
2	*INCOME ITEMS*									
3	allowance	400.00	400.00	400.00	400.00	400.00	400.00	400.00	400.00	400.00
4	part-time work	325.00	325.00	325.00	325.00	325.00	325.00	325.00	325.00	325.00
5	savings withdrawal	333.33	333.33	333.33	333.33	333.33	333.33	333.33	333.33	333.33
6	GROSS INCOME	1058.33	1058.33	1058.33	1058.33	1058.33	1058.33	1058.33	1058.33	1058.33
7										
8	*DEDUCTIONS*									
9	federal income tax (15%)	48.75	48.75	48.75	48.75	48.75	48.75	48.75	48.75	48.75
10	state income tax (4%)	13.00	13.00	13.00	13.00	13.00	13.00	13.00	13.00	13.00
11	FICA (8%)	26.00	26.00	26.00	26.00	26.00	26.00	26.00	26.00	26.00
12	TOTAL DEDUCTIONS	87.75	87.75	87.75	87.75	87.75	87.75	87.75	87.75	87.75
13										
14	**NET INCOME**	970.58	970.58	970.58	970.58	970.58	970.58	970.58	970.58	970.58
15										
16	*FIXED EXPENSE ITEMS*									
17	Rent	350.00	350.00	350.00	350.00	350.00	350.00	350.00	350.00	350.00
18	basic phone service	10.00	10.00	10.00	10.00	10.00	10.00	10.00	10.00	10.00
19	cable television	7.50	7.50	7.50	7.50	7.50	7.50	7.50	7.50	7.50
20	Internet access	5.00	5.00	5.00	5.00	5.00	5.00	5.00	5.00	5.00
21	FIXED EXPENSES	372.50	372.50	372.50	372.50	372.50	372.50	372.50	372.50	372.50
22										
23	*VARIABLE EXP. ITEMS*									
24	groceries/personal items	216.50	216.50	216.50	216.50	216.50	216.50	216.50	216.50	216.50
25	long distance phone calls	25.00	25.00	25.00	25.00	25.00	25.00	25.00	25.00	25.00
26	eating out	125.00	125.00	125.00	125.00	125.00	125.00	125.00	125.00	125.00
27	gasoline	50.00	50.00	50.00	50.00	50.00	50.00	50.00	50.00	50.00
28	school/entertainment	100.00	100.00	100.00	100.00	100.00	100.00	100.00	100.00	100.00
29	VARIABLE EXPENSES	516.50	516.50	516.50	516.50	516.50	516.50	516.50	516.50	516.50
30										
31	**TOTAL EXPENSES**	889.00	889.00	889.00	889.00	889.00	889.00	889.00	889.00	889.00
32										
33	**SURPLUS**	81.58	81.58	81.58	81.58	81.58	81.58	81.58	81.58	81.58

	A	B	C	D	E	F	G	H	I	J
1	ITEM	SEP	OCT	NOV	DEC	JAN	FEB	MAR	APR	MAY
2	*INCOME ITEMS*									
3	Allowance	400.00	400.00	400.00	400.00	400.00	400.00	400.00	400.00	400.00
4	Part-time work	325.00	325.00	325.00	325.00	325.00	325.00	325.00	325.00	325.00
5	savings withdrawal	333.33	333.33	333.33	333.33	333.33	333.33	333.33	333.33	333.33
6	GROSS INCOME	1058.33	1058.33	1058.33	1058.33	1058.33	1058.33	1058.33	1058.33	1058.33
7										
8	*DEDUCTIONS*									
9	federal income tax (15%)	48.75	48.75	48.75	48.75	48.75	48.75	48.75	48.75	48.75
10	state income tax (4%)	13.00	13.00	13.00	13.00	13.00	13.00	13.00	13.00	13.00
11	social security/medicare (8%)	26.00	26.00	26.00	26.00	26.00	26.00	26.00	26.00	26.00
12	TOTAL DEDUCTIONS	87.75	87.75	87.75	87.75	87.75	87.75	87.75	87.75	87.75
13										
14	**NET INCOME**	970.58	970.58	970.58	970.58	970.58	970.58	970.58	970.58	970.58
15										
16	*FIXED EXPENSE ITEMS*									
17	Rent	350.00	350.00	350.00	350.00	350.00	350.00	350.00	350.00	350.00
18	basic phone service	10.00	10.00	10.00	10.00	10.00	10.00	10.00	10.00	10.00
19	cable television	7.50	7.50	7.50	7.50	7.50	7.50	7.50	7.50	7.50
20	Internet access	5.00	5.00	5.00	5.00	5.00	5.00	5.00	5.00	5.00
21	FIXED EXPENSES	372.50	372.50	372.50	372.50	372.50	372.50	372.50	372.50	372.50
22										
23	*VARIABLE EXPENSE ITEMS*									
24	Groceries/personal items	216.50	216.50	216.50	216.50	216.50	216.50	216.50	216.50	216.50
25	long distance phone calls	25.00	25.00	25.00	25.00	25.00	25.00	25.00	25.00	25.00
26	eating out	125.00	125.00	125.00	125.00	125.00	125.00	125.00	125.00	125.00
27	gasoline	50.00	50.00	50.00	50.00	50.00	50.00	50.00	50.00	50.00
28	school/entertainment	100.00	100.00	100.00	100.00	100.00	100.00	100.00	100.00	100.00
29	VARIABLE EXPENSES	516.50	516.50	516.50	516.50	516.50	516.50	516.50	516.50	516.50
30										
31	*PERIODIC EXPENSE ITEMS*									
32	car insurance			600.00						600.00
33	PERIODIC EXPENSES			600.00						600.00
34										
35	**TOTAL EXPENSES**	889.00	889.00	1,489.00	889.00	889.00	889.00	889.00	889.00	1,489.00
36										
37	**SURPLUS**	81.58	81.58	-518.42	81.58	81.58	81.58	81.58	81.58	-518.42

	A	B	C	D	E	F	G	H	I	J
1	ITEM	SEP	OCT	NOV	DEC	JAN	FEB	MAR	APR	MAY
2	INCOME ITEMS									
3	Allowance	400.00	400.00	400.00	400.00	400.00	400.00	400.00	400.00	400.00
4	Part-time work	325.00	325.00	325.00	325.00	325.00	325.00	325.00	325.00	325.00
5	savings withdrawal	333.33	333.33	933.33	333.33	333.33	333.33	333.33	333.33	933.33
6	GROSS INCOME	1058.33	1058.33	1658.33	1058.33	1058.33	1058.33	1058.33	1058.33	1658.33
7										
8	DEDUCTIONS									
9	federal income tax (15%)	48.75	48.75	48.75	48.75	48.75	48.75	48.75	48.75	48.75
10	state income tax (4%)	13.00	13.00	13.00	13.00	13.00	13.00	13.00	13.00	13.00
11	social security/medicare (8%)	26.00	26.00	26.00	26.00	26.00	26.00	26.00	26.00	26.00
12	TOTAL DEDUCTIONS	87.75	87.75	87.75	87.75	87.75	87.75	87.75	87.75	87.75
13										
14	NET INCOME	970.58	970.58	1570.58	970.58	970.58	970.58	970.58	970.58	1570.58
15										
16	FIXED EXPENSE ITEMS									
17	Rent	350.00	350.00	350.00	350.00	350.00	350.00	350.00	350.00	350.00
18	basic phone service	10.00	10.00	10.00	10.00	10.00	10.00	10.00	10.00	10.00
19	cable television	7.50	7.50	7.50	7.50	7.50	7.50	7.50	7.50	7.50
20	Internet access	5.00	5.00	5.00	5.00	5.00	5.00	5.00	5.00	5.00
21	saving	133.33	133.33	133.33	133.33	133.33	133.33	133.33	133.33	133.33
22	FIXED EXPENSES	505.83	505.83	505.83	505.83	505.83	505.83	505.83	505.83	505.83
23										
24	VARIABLE EXPENSE ITEMS									
25	Groceries/personal items	216.50	216.50	216.50	216.50	216.50	216.50	216.50	216.50	216.50
26	long distance phone calls	25.00	25.00	25.00	25.00	25.00	25.00	25.00	25.00	25.00
27	eating out	125.00	125.00	125.00	125.00	125.00	125.00	125.00	125.00	125.00
28	Gasoline	50.00	50.00	50.00	50.00	50.00	50.00	50.00	50.00	50.00
29	school/entertainment	100.00	100.00	100.00	100.00	100.00	100.00	100.00	100.00	100.00
30	VARIABLE EXPENSES	516.50	516.50	516.50	516.50	516.50	516.50	516.50	516.50	516.50
31										
32	PERIODIC EXPENSE ITEMS									
33	car insurance			600.00						600.00
34	PERIODIC EXPENSES			600.00						600.00
35										
36	TOTAL EXPENSES	1022.33	1022.33	1622.33	1022.33	1022.33	1022.33	1022.33	1022.33	1622.33
37										
38	SURPLUS	-51.75	-51.75	-51.75	-51.75	-51.75	-51.75	-51.75	-51.75	-51.75

ITEM	SEP	OCT	NOV	DEC	JAN	FEB	MAR	APR	MAY
INCOME ITEMS									
part-time work	30.00	30.00	30.00	30.00	30.00	30.00	30.00	30.00	30.00
INCOME	30.00	30.00	30.00	30.00	30.00	30.00	30.00	30.00	30.00
FIXED EXPENSE ITEMS									
Save the Rainforest Fund	2.00	2.00	2.00	2.00	2.00	2.00	2.00	2.00	2.00
Loan Repayment	2.78	2.78	2.78	2.78	2.78	2.78	2.78	2.78	2.78
FIXED EXPENSES	4.78	4.78	4.78	4.78	4.78	4.78	4.78	4.78	4.78
VARIABLE EXPENSE ITEMS									
entertainment	10.00	10.00	10.00	10.00	10.00	10.00	10.00	10.00	10.00
food/snacks	5.00	5.00	5.00	5.00	5.00	5.00	5.00	5.00	5.00
clothing	10.00	10.00	10.00	10.00	10.00	10.00	10.00	10.00	10.00
VARIABLE EXPENSES	25.00	25.00	25.00	25.00	25.00	25.00	25.00	25.00	25.00
SAVING	3.00	3.00	3.00	3.00	3.00	3.00	3.00	3.00	3.00
PERIODIC EXPENSE ITEMS									
gifts	5.00	5.00	5.00	5.00	5.00	5.00	5.00	5.00	5.00
water park	8.00	8.00	8.00	8.00	8.00	8.00	8.00	8.00	8.00
PERIODIC EXPENSES	13.00	13.00	13.00	13.00	13.00	13.00	13.00	13.00	13.00
TOTAL EXPENSES	45.78	45.78	45.78	45.78	45.78	45.78	45.78	45.78	45.78
SURPLUS	-15.78	-15.78	-15.78	-15.78	-15.78	-15.78	-15.78	-15.78	-15.78

Money Math (Lesson 4)

Josh,

I think that I can help you. I've prepared a budget spreadsheet for you. That's a list of your monthly income and expenses. It will help you see how much money you have for each month and what your expected expenses are. Right now you have a problem because you have a budget deficit. That means that you are planning to spend more each month than the money you have available. Sometimes people have budget surpluses. That means that they have more money available each month than what they expect to spend. Too bad that's not your problem. If you look at the spreadsheet, you'll see that I have several categories of expenses. Fixed expenses don't vary from month to month. For you, the donation to the rainforest fund is a fixed expense. Since you're my good friend, I've decided you can pay part of the $25 you owe me each month. Then it won't be so hard. That payment is also a fixed expense. You also have some variable expenses. These expenses can change from month to month. For example, one month you might spend more for food or clothing than in another month. You also have some periodic expenses. These occur once in a while. The trip to the water park and gifts for holidays are periodic expenses. I also included the saving your mother recommended. It's only $3 per month. That's not so bad. If you look at the entire spreadsheet, you'll notice that you only have $30 to spend each month. There are 9 months in the school year so I divided $270 by 9. However, you expect to spend $45.78 each month. You can't do that. You don't have enough money.

I have some suggestions that might help you balance your budget. That means your expenses equal the amount of money you have to spend. To do that, you have to reduce what you spend and/or increase your income. You can reduce the amount you want each month for clothes. Your old jeans still fit, so you can get by with one pair of Frumpy and Fitch jeans. You'll only need $5 each month for clothes. Also, you can make gifts instead of buying gifts. You'll only need $2 each month for gifts. You could also reduce the amount you spend at the water park if you bring some snacks from home and play fewer video games. You'll only need $7 each month. Finally, I think you better plan on shoveling snow and babysitting each month. Maybe you could be a soccer referee for the little kids' soccer program at the community center, too. That will give you some additional income. I bet you can earn about $15 a month. You could also ask your grandparents for money for your birthday. That would help. You might end up with extra spending money for the trip!